THE THAMES

NATIONAL TRAIL

COMPANION

supported by

3rd edition published February 2003

© National Trails Office

ISBN 0-9535207-4-9

edited by Rebecca Wilson & Jos Joslin

Photographs on pages 4, 6, 20, 28, 36, 37, 46, 54, 56, 58, 59, 69, 71, 90 top, 95, 96 and 102 by Rob Fraser;

Photographs on the cover and pages 11, 15, 18, 27, 30, 38, 47, 49, 55, 61, 74, 76, 79, 81, 82, 93 and 98 by Jos Joslin

Published by National Trails Office

Cultural Services

Holton

Oxford OX33 1QQ

tel 01865 810224

fax 01865 810207

email mail@rway-tpath.demon.co.uk

website www.nationaltrail.co.uk

Produced by Leap Frog, a division of Promotional Print Ltd.

tel 01484 726620

Designed by Linda Francis

cover photo by Jos Joslin

Swans near Swinford, upstream of Oxford

Contents

The Rose Revived Inn, Newbridge

Introduction

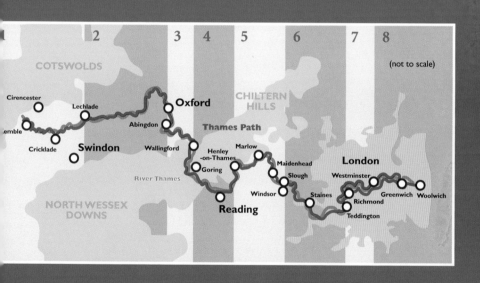

The Thames Path follows England's best known river for 294 km (184 miles) as it meanders from its source in Gloucestershire through several rural counties and on into the bustle of the City of London. On its way the Path passes peaceful water meadows rich in wildlife, historic towns and many lovely villages, finishing at the Thames Barrier in Woolwich. Easy to reach by public transport, the Thames Path is accessible for walkers of all ages and abilities. This National Trail can be enjoyed in many ways, whether for an afternoon's stroll, a weekend's break or a full scale, but relatively gentle, trek of its whole length.

Windsor Castle

Welcome to the Thames Path Companion. It provides up-to-date practical information about accommodation, refreshments and many other facilities along the 294 km (184 miles) of National Trail from the source of the river in Gloucestershire, through Wiltshire, Oxfordshire, Berkshire, Buckinghamshire, Surrey and into London. The Companion is designed to help with planning anything from a three week's walking holiday to an afternoon out with the dog.

The Companion is not a route guide: for detailed information of the Trail itself, *The Thames Path National Trail Guide* by David Sharp is available from most book shops. Alternatively it can be mail ordered from the National Trails Office (see page 17 for details). The Companion complements the Trail Guide and, armed with a copy of each, it is hoped that anyone using the Trail needn't require anything more. Enjoy your trip.

Opened in 1996 as one of thirteen National Trails in England, the Thames Path follows the country's best known river as it meanders from its source in the Cotswolds through several rural counties and on into the heart of London. This Trail provides level, easy walking and can be enjoyed in many ways, whether for an afternoon's stroll, a weekend's break or a full scale, but relatively gentle trek of its whole length. Another advantage is that the Thames Path can be easily reached by public transport, including an excellent network of train services the whole distance between Oxford and London.

At the start of the Path, the source of the River Thames beneath an elderly ash tree in a field in the Cotswolds, you may well find no water at all. However, gradually as you travel the trickle becomes a stream and soon a river bordered by willows and alders. As far as Oxford, apart from a couple of small historic towns and a few pleasant villages, there is a real sense of remoteness and rural tranquillity as the Thames winds its way through flat water meadows grazed by cattle or sheep, or fields of crops.

i INTRODUCTION

Beyond Oxford, the city of dreaming spires, you will still be in the heart of the countryside with its wealth of wildlife. The river whose banks you're following continues to widen, the willows seem to grow larger, and settlements become more frequent. From Goring where the Path coincides for a short distance with another National Trail, the ancient Ridgeway, the Chiltern Hills provide a wooded backdrop to your journey with their colours changing dramatically with the seasons.

When you reach Henley the Path starts to get busier with more people enjoying strolls with a dog, picnics on the bank or boating trips on the water. However, once you're away from towns or villages around a bend or two of the river, you'll regain the rural peacefulness. As the Thames Path passes beneath Windsor Castle, you are reminded that you are following a Royal river; the palaces of Hampton Court and Kew a little further downstream confirm this.

From the last non-tidal lock on the Thames at Teddington, you can choose to walk on either the north or the south bank of the river through most of London. You'll pass leafy Richmond and Kew, remarkably green areas, before entering the heart of the City with its many famous buildings bordering the Thames. The final few kilometres to the finish at the Thames Barrier take you amongst restored warehouses and the working wharves in London's Docklands.

With the support of the Countryside Agency, the Thames Path is managed to the highest standards necessary for one of the most important paths in the country by the local highway authorities with a small dedicated team of National Trails staff and volunteers.

The Thames Valley was originally settled by prehistoric people with the earliest occupations discovered so far dating from the New Stone Age, some 6 000 years ago. These are at Runnymede and Staines near the Thames, not far from present day London. The river has been a very important trading route for hundreds of years and it is really only during the latter half of the twentieth century that it mostly ceased to carry goods. Nowadays leisure boats rather than barges are the main users of the Thames.

It was in medieval times that the river became increasingly important for trade, especially in those days for carrying wool from the lush Cotswold meadows to London. St Paul's Cathedral is built of Taynton stone quarried in the Cotswolds and carried to London by barges towed by men and horses from Radcot. By the 18th century London was the world's busiest port and Reading, for example, received 95% of its goods by barge towed along the River Thames.

The towpath between Lechlade and Putney, along which much of the Thames Path now travels, was established towards the end of the 18th century by the Thames Commissioners at a time when the country's new canal system was being built which connected the Thames to other parts of Britain. It was a difficult task since many landowners refused permission for the towing path to enter their land or there were natural obstacles in its way. As a result in many places the towpath switched from one bank of the river to the other and ferries were used to transfer the towing horses across the river. When the commercial traffic died as a result of competition from the railways so did the navigation ferries.

This created a major problem for the setting up of the Thames Path. Either bridges had to be built where the old ferries used to operate or alternative routes to the towpath had to be found.

Wherever you walk along the Thames Path there should be plenty of wildlife to observe and enjoy although, of course, the time of year you are there is important. There will be birds present all year round, but if you're keen on wild flowers then April to September is the time to visit, and if insects are an interest of yours choose June to September.

Plants of the riverside seem to be especially colourful from the bright yellow of the flag iris and marsh marigold in spring to the pinks of the willowherbs and purple loosestrife during summer. Plants of particular note along the Path are the nationally rare Loddon lily and snake's-head fritillary, both flowering on a few flood meadows in early spring.

Insects are in abundance during the summer when dragonflies and damselflies, amongst the largest and so most noticeable, are active. There are various species, many wonderfully coloured and you'll be able to watch them mating, laying eggs, hunting for food or patrolling their territories.

Snakeshead-fritillaries

Of the mammals you'll no doubt see rabbits and maybe a stoat or a weasel. Unfortunately you're unlikely to see a relative of the latter, an otter, although thankfully they are returning to the upper reaches of the Thames and perhaps in the future will be more plentiful and obvious. Another animal in trouble is the water vole, 'Ratty' of Kenneth Grahame's 'Wind in the Willows'. They used to be very common on the Thames emerging from their holes in the bank and busily ploughing backwards and forwards across the river, but their numbers have crashed in recent years. Let us know if and where you spot one.

The most obvious animals are the birds, many of which being water birds are large and thankfully don't fly away as soon as you appear! The majestic mute swan has to be the symbol of the Thames and is increasingly common thanks to the ban in the 1980s on anglers using lead weights. Swans eating these weights in mistake for the grit they need to take in to break down plant material in their gizzards were poisoned and killed and their numbers diminished considerably.

Wherever you go you'll see the commonest of Britain's ducks, the mallard, which like all ducks is especially resplendent from October to March. But other species of ducks visit the river too, so look out for tufted duck, pochard and wigeon. Geese, larger relatives of ducks, also abound in places, usually found in large noisy flocks grazing in fields near the river or roosting on the water itself. The Canada goose is very common.

The Thames Path is primarily a route for use by walkers, although in a few places, especially in towns and cities and near London, cyclists can use sections. In a few places horseriders, too, can share the Path.

Spring, summer and autumn months are the best time to enjoy the Thames Path since there is very little risk of the river flooding and making the Trail impassable.

Be prepared!

Whenever venturing into the countryside it is wise to be prepared for the elements: even in summer, wind and rain can make a walk cold and uncomfortable, so suitable warm and waterproof clothing should be worn or carried in a small rucksack. After rain, and particularly during winter, the Trail can be muddy, so wear strong, comfortable and waterproof footwear.

During winter months and occasionally at other times, some sections of the Path, especially in the upper reaches, can become flooded and unwalkable after heavy rain. To be sure of keeping your feet dry telephone the **Environment Agency's flood information line on 08459 881188.**

Dog Matters

If you are planning to undertake a long distance walk along the Thames Path with your dog, you are advised to ensure it is fit before you start; on occasions walkers have had to abandon a walk because their dogs can't keep up!

Please also make sure your dog is under close control at all times to prevent it from disturbing livestock or wildlife. Whilst in fields with livestock you are asked to keep your dog on a lead, although on occasions cattle may harass you because of the dog and in such circumstances it may be wise to let it off the lead.

Signing

The Thames Path follows a series of well-signed public rights of way along which people have a legal right of access.

An acorn, the symbol of Britain's National Trails, is used to guide your journey by marking the route in a variety of ways. It is used in conjunction with coloured arrows or the words 'footpath', 'bridleway' or 'byway' to indicate who can use a particular right of way.

The word 'footpath' and/or a yellow arrow indicates a path for use by walkers only and where, without the landowner's permission, it is illegal to cycle, ride a horse or drive a vehicle. Outside London, 83% of the Thames Path is footpath.

The word 'bridleway' and/or a blue arrow indicates a path which can be used by walkers, horseriders and cyclists but where, without the landowner's permission, it is illegal to drive any vehicle. Outside London, 6% of the Thames Path is bridleway.

The word 'byway' and/or a red arrow indicates a right of way which can be legally used by walkers, horseriders, cyclists and motorists. Outside London, 0.7% of the Thames Path is byway.

The Thames Path is signposted where it crosses roads and many rights of way using wooden or metal signposts. Elsewhere, waymark discs with acorns and coloured arrows are used on gates, stiles and waymark posts.

Guides

The Thames Path National Trail Guide by David Sharp, Aurum Press – the official Guide with written route description and colour maps.

Maps

It is always a good idea to use an Ordnance Survey map when walking, particularly in unfamiliar areas. The National Trail Guide includes colour sections of all the appropriate 1:25 000 maps needed to follow the Thames Path. Alternatively, for you to enjoy and interpret the wider landscape, you may wish to purchase your own maps.

The Landranger series (pink cover at 1:50 000 or 2 cm to 1 km) has all public rights of way, viewpoints, tourist information and selected places of interest marked on them. For the whole of the Path you will need:

163   Cheltenham & Cirencester
164   Oxford
174   Newbury and Wantage
175   Reading and Windsor
176   West London
177   East London

The larger scale Explorer series (orange cover at 1:25 000 or 4 cm to 1 km) has more detail including fence lines which can be very helpful when following rights of way, recreational routes and greater tourist information. For the whole of the Path you will need:

FINDING YOUR WAY   v

Opposite Port Meadow, Oxford

vi PUBLICATIONS

Publications about the Thames Path and River

There are many publications available about the River Thames and its Path of which the following is a selection:

The Thames Path National Trail Guide by David Sharp, Aurum Press 2001 – the official guide with written route description and colour maps.

Thames: the River and the Path Geoprojects 2002 – a fold-out map at a scale of 1:60 000.

Walks Along the Thames Path by Ron Emmons, 2001 – 25 circular walks from Thames Head to Greenwich.

The Thames Path by Leigh Hatts, Cicerone Press 2000

Pubs of the River Thames by Mark Turner, Prion Books 2000 – colour pictures and details of over 100 pubs beside the Thames from the Cotswolds to London's East End.

Rambling for Pleasure along the Thames East Berkshire Ramblers Group 1999 – short circular walks (all less than 6 miles) between Runnymede and Sonning.

Pub Walks along the Thames Path by Leigh Hatts, Countryside Books 1997 – 20 circular walks.

The Secret Thames by Duncan Mackay, Ebury Press/Countryside Commission 1996

Chilterns and Thames Valley Walks Ordnance Survey Pathfinder Guide 1994

The Thames Path by Helen Livingstone, Aerofilms Guide 1993 – aerial photographs illustrate the route of the path.

Walks along the Thames Path by Leigh Hatts, Patrick Stephens Ltd 1990 – circular walks incorporating the Thames Path.

A Walk along the River Thames by Gareth Huw Davies, Michael Joseph 1990

Sea to Source – London Weekend Television 2002 – VHS video **T:** 0871 220 9949

World's Most Beautiful Waterways – *The Thames* Contender Entertainment 2000 – VHS video, introduced by David Suchet

Thames Path Manager

National Trails Officers, Mike Furness and Jos Joslin, National Trails Office, Cultural Services, Holton, Oxford OX33 1QQ **T:** 01865 810224
F: 01865 810207 **E:** mail@rway-tpath.demon.co.uk

Highway Authorities responsible for public rights of way

Buckinghamshire County Council, Environmental Services Dept, County Hall, Walton Street, AYLESBURY HP20 1UY **T:** 01296 395000 www.buckscc.gov.uk

Gloucestershire County Council, Environment Dept, Shire Hall, Westgate Street, GLOUCESTER GL1 2TH **T:** 01452 425500 www.gloscc.gov.uk

Oxfordshire County Council, Countryside Service, Cultural Services, Holton, OXFORD OX33 1QQ **T:** 01865 810226 www.oxfordshire.gov.uk

Reading Borough Council, Leisure Services, Civic Offices, Civic Centre, READING RG1 7TD **T:** 01189 390900 www.reading.gov.uk

Royal Borough of Windsor and Maidenhead, Planning and Environment, Town Hall, St Ives Road, MAIDENHEAD SL6 1RF **T:** 01628 798888 www.rbwm.gov.uk

Surrey County Council, Environment, County Hall, KINGSTON KT1 2DY **T:** 08456 009 009 www.surreycc.gov.uk

Swindon Borough Council, Borough Engineer's Dept, Premier House, Station Road, SWINDON SN1 1TZ **T:** 01793 463000 www.swindon.gov.uk

West Berkshire Council, Environment and Countryside, Faraday Road, NEWBURY RG14 2AF **T:** 01635 42400 www.westberks.gov.uk

Wiltshire County Council, Dept of Environmental Services, County Hall, TROWBRIDGE, BA14 8JN **T:** 01225 713000 www.wiltshire.gov.uk

Wokingham Unitary, Environment Services, Shute End Offices, WOKINGHAM RG40 1GY **T:** 01189 778731 www.wokingham.gov.uk

vii **USEFUL CONTACTS**

Agency responsible for National Trails

Countryside Agency, Dacre House, 19 Dacre Street, LONDON SW1H 0DH
T: 020 7340 2900   www.countryside.gov.uk

Agency responsible for the River Thames

Environment Agency, Kings Meadow House, Kings Meadow Road,
READING RG1 8DQ **T**: 0118 953500 www.environment-agency.gov.uk

Environment Agency's Flood Information **T**: 08459 881188

Weathercall (up-to-date weather forecasts)

	Telephone Numbers
Section One (Wiltshire and Gloucestershire)	09068 505305
Sections Two, Three, Four and Five (Oxfordshire, Berkshire and Buckinghamshire)	09068 505306
Section Six (Surrey)	09068 505302
Sections Seven and Eight (London)	09068 505301

OR www.met-office.gov.uk (The areas covering the Thames Path are:
South-East England & the West Country)

Just upstream from Hambleden Lo

The Thames Path is exceptionally well served by public transport which makes it possible to explore the Trail without needing a car by using trains, buses or, unusually for a National Trail, boats.

A free leaflet summarising the bus, train and boat services to the Trail is available from the National Trails Office (see page 17 for details).

Rail Services

For information:
National Rail Enquiries **T**: 08457 484950 (24 hours a day)
www.nationalrail.co.uk or www.railtrack.co.uk for timetables

Thames Trains operating trains between London, Reading and Oxford stopping at a further eight stations close to the Path (Tilehurst, Pangbourne, Goring, Cholsey, Culham, and Radley and the branch lines from Maidenhead and Twyford) issues a special ticket for walkers. Ask for a Thames Path Cheap Day Return ticket to the furthest point of your walk and it covers you automatically for the return journey on the same day from another Thames Trains station.

Bus Services

For information:
National Public Transport Information Service **T**: 0870 608 2608
www.pti.org.uk

Public Transport in London

For information:
London Travel Information **T**: 020 7222 1234
www.londontransport.co.uk

Details of taxi services are included at the beginning of each section.

19

• Enjoy the countryside, but remember that most of the Thames Path crosses private farmland and estates which are living and working landscapes.

• Always keep to the Path to avoid trespass and use gates and stiles to negotiate fences and hedges.

• Crops and animals are the farmer's livelihood – please leave them alone.

• To avoid injury or distress to farm animals and wildlife, keep your dogs under close control at all times – preferably on a lead through fields with farm animals. (NB: If you are concerned that cattle are harassing you, it may be safer to let your dog off the lead.)

• Remember to leave things as they are – fasten those gates you find closed. Straying farm animals can cause damage and inconvenience.

• Please take your litter home, otherwise it can injure people and animals and looks unsightly.

• Guard against all risk of fires especially in dry weather.

• Take special care on country roads and, if travelling by car, park sensibly so as not to obstruct others or gateways.

Ponies grazing on Port Meadow, Oxford

In emergency dial 999 and ask for the service required.

Police

To contact local police stations, telephone the number relevant to the section/county you are in and ask to be put through to the nearest police station.

Section	County	Telephone Numbers
1	Gloucestershire	08450 090 1234
	Wiltshire	01380 735735
2	Gloucestershire	08450 090 1234
	Oxfordshire	01865 846000
3	Oxfordshire	01865 846000
4	Oxfordshire & Berkshire	01865 846000
5	Berkshire & Buckinghamshire	01865 846000
6	Berkshire	01865 846000
	Surrey	01483 555111
7	Surrey	01483 555111
	Greater London	020 7230 1212
8	Greater London	020 7230 1212
	City of London	020 7601 2222
		or 0800 28 2806
		(within City area only)

Hospitals

The following hospital with casualty departments are located in the places shown below. The telephone numbers given are for the hospital switchboard; ask to be put through to Accident & Emergency Reception.

◆ Full 24-hour emergency service

▼ Minor injuries only, 24-hour service

Section	Town/City	Telephone No	Address
1	◆ Cirencester	01285 655711	Cirencester Hospital, the Querns, Tetbury Road, Cirencester
	◆ Swindon	01793 536231	Princess Margaret Hospital, Okus Road, Swindon
2	◆ Swindon	01793 536231	Princess Margaret Hospital, Okus Road, Swindon
	◆ Oxford	01865 741166	John Radcliffe Hospital, Headley Way, Headington, Oxford
3	◆ Oxford	01865 741166	John Radcliffe Hospital, Headley Way, Headington, Oxford
	◆ Wallingford	01491 698500	Wallingford Community Hospital, Reading Road, Wallingford
4	◆ Wallingford	01491 698500	Wallingford Community Hospital, Reading Road, Wallingford
	◆ Reading	0118 987 5111	The Royal Berkshire Hospital, London Road, Reading
	▼ Henley	01491 572544	Townlands Hospital, York Rd, Henley

5	▼ Henley	01491 572544	Townlands Hospital, York Road, Henley
	◆ High Wycombe	01494 526161	Wycombe General Hospital, Queen Alexandra Road, High Wycombe
6	◆ Slough	01753 633000	Wexham Park Hospital, Wexham Street, Slough
	◆ Chertsey	01932 872000	St Peter's Hospital, Guildford Road, Chertsey
	◆ Kingston upon Thames	020 8546 7711	Kingston Hospital, Galsworthy Road, Kingston upon Thames
7	◆ Isleworth	020 8560 2121	West Middlesex University Hospital, Twickenham Road, Isleworth
	◆ Hammersmith	020 8846 1234	Charing Cross Hospital, Fulham Palace Road, Hammersmith, London W6
	◆ Kensington	020 8746 8000	Chelsea & Westminster Hospital, 369 Fulham Road, Kensington, London SW10
8	◆ Vauxhall	020 7928 9292	St Thomas's Hospital, Lambeth Palace Road, Vauxhall, London SE1
	◆ The City	020 7955 5000	Guy's Hospital, St Thomas Street, Strand, London SE1
	◆ Dartford	01322 428100	Darenth Valley Hospital, Darenth Wood Road, Dartford

Accommodation, Facilities & Services

This booklet gives details of the settlements, accommodation, eating places, shops, attractions and other facilities along the Thames Path. They are listed in geographic order from the source of the river to the Thames Barrier in London.

If you fail to find accommodation using this guide please contact the Tourist Information Centres listed near the beginning of each section which may be able to provide other addresses. Some towns and cities, including London, have such an extensive range and number of places to stay that details of individual establishments are not listed in this guide.

The Thames Path is divided into eight sections as indicated on the map on page 5. At the start of each section is a map showing the settlements close to the Trail within that section. These maps are meant only as a guide and you are recommended to use this Companion in conjunction with The Thames Path National Trail Guide or maps.

You are strongly advised to book accommodation in advance, and during summer as early as possible. Whilst booking, do check prices since those quoted here are usually the minimum charged.

For those who would like to enjoy more than a day on the Thames Path without having to carry all their possessions, quite a few accommodation providers have indicated whether they are willing to transport the luggage you don't need during the day to your next night's accommodation. The fee charged for this service needs to be discussed and agreed at the time of the booking. Accommodation providers have also indicated if they are willing to collect you from the Thames Path and deliver you back after your stay.

All the information within this Companion is as accurate as possible. Inclusion of accommodation does not constitute a recommendation although it is indicated in the details whether an establishment has a recognised grade awarded to it. If you have any comments or notice any errors, please write to Jos Joslin the National Trails Officer responsible for this guide (page 17).

Key to Symbols for Settlements

Any comments relate to preceding icon.

⊹   map grid reference (see start of each section for relevant maps)

👢   shortest walking distance from the Thames Path

🚆   most convenient train station

📞   telephone

🚻   toilets

♿WC   toilets adapted for disabled users

ℹ️   Tourist Information Centre

🍺   pub (usually open lunchtimes 11am-3pm then evenings 6pm-11pm)

✕   bar meals in pub

✉️   post office (usual opening hours 9am-5.30pm weekdays; 9am-12.30pm Sat)

🧺   general store (usual opening hours 9am-5.30pm Mon-Sat)

☕   cafe/tea shop

🍽️   restaurant

🥡   food take-away

▯▯▯▯▯▯▯▯ opening hours of services relate to the preceding symbol
S M T W T F S

eg: ▯ open all day   ▮ closed all day

      ▯ Post offices, general stores,   ▮ Post offices, general stores,
         cafe/tea shops – open morning;   cafe/tea shops – open afternoon;
         Pubs, bar meals, restaurants,   Pubs, bar meals, restaurants,
         takeaways – open lunchtimes   takeaways – open evening

£   bank (usually open daily 9.30am-4.30pm Mon-Fri)

▦   cash machine available including outside bank opening hours

☆   tourist attraction

Key to Symbols for Accommodation

Type of accommodation (symbols in margins)

🛖	youth hostel	Ⓗ	hotel
⛺	camping	INN	inn

The number and price following the symbols for rooms gives the number and price of that type of room available. The same applies to tent/caravan pitches. Prices quoted for rooms are the minimum price per room per night for bed and breakfast. The price for single occupancy of double, twin or family rooms is given in brackets eg (£22.00).

Accommodation symbols – hotels, inns, guest houses, B&Bs and youth hostels

🛏	double room	DRY	clothes/boots drying facilities
🛏	twin room	⊙	laundry facilities
🛏	family room	🚗	transport to and from Trail by arrangement
🛏	single room		
⊘	no smoking in bedrooms	🚶	luggage transported to next overnight stop by arrangement
🚻	children welcome	VISA	credit card(s) accepted
♿	wheelchair access		
🐕	dogs allowed by arrangement	◆	English Tourism Council grade for B&Bs, guest houses, inns
V	caters for vegetarians	★	English Tourism Council grade for hotels
🍴	packed lunches available		
⊘	evening meals available at accommodation or locally	🎭	special feature/comment

Accommodation symbols – camping and caravan sites

⛺	tent pitches	🚿	showers
🚐	caravan pitches	☎	public telephone
⚖	cold water	⬚	laundry facilities
⚖	hot water	🏪	site shop
⊛	toilets	CG	camping gas available
&WC	toilets adapted for disabled users	▮	special feature/comment

Kelmscot

27

Ha'penny Bridge, Lechlade

Section 1

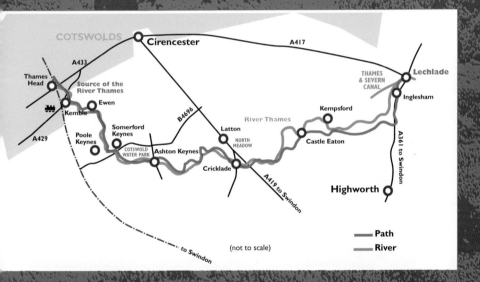

The Source to Lechlade

This rural first 37 km (23 miles) of the Thames Path is within the fine countryside of the Cotswolds where farming and small village communities dominate. The river you follow grows from nothing to a trickle to a respectable body of water by the time you reach Lechlade.

The source of the Thames at the start of this section lies in a remote Gloucestershire meadow beneath the boughs of an elderly ash tree. For much of the year this spring is dry and, especially if you're walking during the summer, you may find the bed of the Thames remains without water for some distance.

Your route following the infant river wanders through fields and through or near to several small Cotswold villages characterised by creamy stonework buildings with stone slate roofs. These are ideal places to enjoy a refreshment stop.

Before you reach the small, originally Saxon, town of Cricklade where the right of upstream navigation ends, you'll pass through the middle of the Cotswold Water Park and its blue landscape of gravel extracted lagoons. Just outside Cricklade the Path skirts around the edge of North Meadow where, usually towards the end of April, the rare snake's-head fritillary flowers in vast numbers.

At Inglesham the flow of the Thames is increased by the water of the River Coln which joins it. The church and Round House here are worth seeing before you walk on into Lechlade.

Close to the Source of the Thames

Maps

Landranger maps	163	Cheltenham and Gloucester
Explorer maps	168	Stroud, Tetbury and Malmesbury
	169	Cirencester and Swindon
	170	Abingdon, Wantage and Vale of White Horse

Transport Information

Rail Services	National Rail **T**: 08457 484950 or www.nationalrail.co.uk or www.railtrack.co.uk
Bus Services	National Public Transport Information Service **T**: 0870 608 2608 or www.pti.org.uk

Taxi Services

Place	Name	Telephone numbers
Cirencester	Alma Travel	01285 644584
	Cirencester Taxis	01285 642767
	Monarch Taxis	01285 656871
Kemble	Station Taxis	01285 770717
Lechlade	CTs	01367 252575

Toilets at Locks

St John's Lock, Lechlade

Police

Gloucestershire	**T**: 01242 521321
Wiltshire	**T**: 01793 528111

1 A Taster

Hospitals

Cirencester	Cirencester Hospital, The Querns, Tetbury Road, Cirencester **T:** 01285 655711
Swindon	Princess Margaret Hospital, Okus Road, Swindon **T:** 01793 536231

Tourist Information Centres

Both provide an accommodation booking service.

Place	Address/Opening Hours
Cirencester	Corn Hall, Market Place, Cirencester GL7 2NW **T:** 01285 654180 **F:** 01285 641182 **Opening hours** Summer (Apr-end Dec): Mon 9:45-17:30, Tue-Sat 9:30-17:30 Winter (Jan-end Mar): Mon 9:45-17:00, Tue-Sat 9:30-17:00
Swindon	37 Regent Street, Swindon SN1 1JL **T:** 01793 530328 **F:** 01793 434031 **E:** infocentre@swindon.gov.uk www. visitswindon.co.uk **Opening hours** All year: Mon-Sat 9:15-17:00

View of Ewen from the river

CIRENCESTER

 SP0201 ⌂ 5km (3miles)

🚂 Kemble 8km (5miles)

Town with full range of services

☆ Corinium Museum **T:** 01285 655611

☆ Brewery Arts **T:** 01285 657181

☆ Roman Amphitheatre **T:** 01179 750700

Cirencester has a wide range of accommodation; details can be obtained from the Tourist Information Centre. However, the accommodation provider below particularly welcomes Thames Path walkers.

Sunset	April - September

Mrs J E Castle
Baunton Lane, CIRENCESTER, GL7 2NQ
T: 01285 654822

🛏 1 £34.00 🛏 2 £17.00 👫 (min age 5)
V 🌀 🚭 **DRY** 🚗 👣 ◆◆◆

THAMES HEAD

 SU9898 ⌂ on path

🚂 Kemble 2km (1.2miles)

KEMBLE

 ST9897 ⌂ 1km (0.5miles)

🚂 Kemble 📞

Smerrill Barns	Closed Xmas

Mrs Gabrielle Sopher
Kemble, CIRENCESTER, GL7 6BW
T: 01285 770907 **M:** 07973 840101
F: 01285 770706 **E:** gsopher@hotmail.com
www.smerrillbarns.com

🛏 5 £55.00 🥾 1 £55.00 (£45.00)
🛏 1 £80.00 👫 🖼 V 🌀 🚭 **DRY** 📷 🚗
💳 Visa, Mastercard, Delta ◆◆◆◆

1   The Source to Lechlade

EWEN

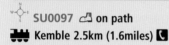

SU0097 ⌂ on path

🚂 Kemble 2.5km (1.6miles) 📞

🍺 |||||||||||| S M T W T F S ✕ |||||||||||| S M T W T F S

☆ Cirencester Park **T:** 01285 653135

Brooklands Farm

Mrs Betty Crew

Ewen, CIRENCESTER, GL7 6BU

T: 01285 770487 **F:** 01285 770487

 2 £40.00 (£25.00) 🛏️ 🚫 🚗 🚶

◆◆◆◆

SOMERFORD KEYNES

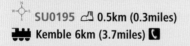

SU0195 ⌂ 0.5km (0.3miles)

🚂 Kemble 6km (3.7miles) 📞

🍺 |||||||||||| S M T W T F S ✕ |||||||||||| S M T W T F S

☆ Cotswold Water Park **T:** 01285 861459
www.waterpark.org

POOLE KEYNES

SU0095 ⌂ 1.3km (0.8miles)

🚂 Kemble 4km (2.5miles) 📞

Willow Pool

Mrs Vivienne Jones

Oaksey Road, Cotswold Water Park,
CIRENCESTER, GL7 6DZ

T: 01285 861485 **M:** 07980 501049

E: jones.willow@btopenworld.com

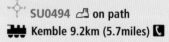 1 £46.00 🛏️ (£28.00)1 £46.00

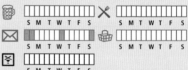 1 £60.00 ♟ V ♿ 🚫 DRY 🚗

◆◆◆◆ ♿ ETC Silver Award, en-suite
rooms, waterfront position, brochure available

ASHTON KEYNES

SU0494 ⌂ on path

🚂 Kemble 9.2km (5.7miles) 📞

🍺 |||||||||||| S M T W T F S ✕ |||||||||||| S M T W T F S

✉ |||||||||||| S M T W T F S 🧺 |||||||||||| S M T W T F S

🎫 |||||||||||| S M T W T F S

☆ Cotswold Water Park **T:** 01285 861459
www.waterpark.org

*The Thames in
Gloucestershire*

~ *Wheatleys Farm* ~

A new traditionally built farmhouse on a 500 acre dairy farm. On the outskirts of the picturesque village of Ashton Keynes in the Cotswold Water Park. Two ensuite rooms. Two pubs with restaurants approx. 5 mins walking distance.

Tel Gill Freeth 01285 861310

Cove House

Mrs V B Threlfall
1 Cove House, Ashton Keynes, SWINDON, SN6 6NS
T: 01285 861226 **F:** 01285 861226
E: Roger@covehouse.co.uk
🛏 1 £58.00 🛏 1 £56.00 (£35.00)
♟V ⚠ 🚫 DRY ⭕ 👣

Wheatleys Farm

Gill Freeth
High Road, Ashton Keynes, SWINDON, SN6 6NX
T: 01285 861310 **M:** 07779 684260
F: 01285 861310
E: wheatleys.farm@lineone.net
www.smoothhound.co.uk/a55176.html
🛏 1 £50.00 (£35.00) 🛏 1 £75.00 ♟
V ⚠ 🚫 DRY ⭕ 🚗 👣 ◆◆◆◆
🅷 All rooms en-suite

1 The Source to Lechlade

LATTON

SU0995 ⌂ 2.5km (1.6miles)

🚂 Swindon 15km (9.3miles) 📞

Dolls House

Mrs Jemma Maraffi
Latton, CRICKLADE, SN6 6DJ
T: 01793 750384 **M:** 07762 619049
F: 01793 750384
E: info@dollshousecricklade.co.uk
www.dollshousecricklade.co.uk
🛏 1 £47.00 🛏 1 £47.00 (£29.00)
🛏 1 £29.00 ♕ (min age 14) 📺 V 🚭
DRY 📷 🚗 👟 💳 Visa, Mastercard,
Delta ◆◆◆ ⚓ ETC Silver Award

Cottages in Cricklade

CRICKLADE

SU0993 ⌂ on path

🚂 Swindon 12.5km (7.8miles) 📞 ♿WC

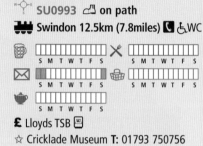

£ Lloyds TSB 🏧
☆ Cricklade Museum **T:** 01793 750756

☆ North Meadow National Nature
Reserve **T:** 01380 726334
www.english-nature.org.uk

☆ Swindon & Cricklade Railway. Open Sat
& Sun only. **T:** 01793 771615
www.swindon-cricklade-railway.org.uk

The White Hart Hotel   *closed Xmas* Ⓗ

Mr Bill Finch
High Street, CRICKLADE, SN6 6AA
T: 01793 750206 **F:** 01793 750650
E: bill@whitehart-cricklade.com
www.the-whitehart-hotel.co.uk
🛏 3 £65.00 🛏 5 £65.00 (£45.00)
🛏 2 £90.00 🛏 2 £45.00 ♕V 🚭 🐾 🚫
💳 Visa, Mastercard, American Express,
Delta ★★ ⚓ Luggage transport can be
arranged through local taxi firm

CASTLE EATON

SU1495 🥾 on path

🚂 Swindon 13.8km (8.6miles) 📞

🍺 | S M T W T F S | ✕ | S M T W T F S |

✉ | S M T W T F S |

⛺ **Second Chance Touring Park**   *closed Dec – Feb*

Mrs B Stroud
Marston Meysey, SWINDON, SN6 6SZ
T: 01285 810675/810939
⛺ 26 £8.00 🚐 26 £8.00 🚿 🚿 ♿ 🖥
CG 🥾 Reached by crossing Castle Eaton
Bridge

KEMPSFORD

SU1696 🥾 1.8km (1.1miles)

🚂 Swindon 18km (11.2miles) 📞

🍺 | S M T W T F S | ✕ | S M T W T F S |

✉ | S M T W T F S |

Kempsford Manor

Mrs Z I Williamson
FAIRFORD, GL7 4EQ
T: 01285 810131
http://members.lycos.co.uk/kempsford_
manor
🛏 2 £55.00 (£30.00) 🛏 1 £30.00 👫
🖤 V 🔥 🚭 🚫 DRY 🖥 🚗 ◆◆◆
🥾 10% discount on 2 nights + transport

Downstream of Cricklade

LECHLADE

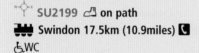

⊹ SU2199 🛶 on path

🚂 Swindon 17.5km (10.9miles) 📞

♿WC

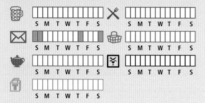

	S	M	T	W	T	F	S
🍺							

	S	M	T	W	T	F	S
✉							

	S	M	T	W	T	F	S
☕							

	S	M	T	W	T	F	S
🎁							

	S	M	T	W	T	F	S
✕							

	S	M	T	W	T	F	S
🧺							

	S	M	T	W	T	F	S
🏆							

£ Barclays

☆ Lechlade Trout Farm T: 01367 253266

🏨 New Inn Hotel

Mr Nick Sandhu

Market Square, LECHLADE, GL7 3AB

T: 01367 252296 F: 01367 252315

E: info@newinnhotel.com

www.newinnhotel.com

🛏 10 £45.00 🛏 15 £45.00 (£45.00)

🛏 2 £50.00 🛏 10 £40.00 ⛹ (min age 5)

♿ 🖼 V 🐾 🚭 🚫 DRY 🗜 🚗 🚶 VISA

Visa, Mastercard, American Express, Delta

★★★

Bridge House Camp Site   *closed Nov - Feb* ⛺

Mr R Cooper

Bridge House, LECHLADE, GL7 3AG

T: 01367 252348 F: 01367 252348

⛺ 40 £7.00 🚐 11 £9.00 🖼 🐾 🐕

♿WC 🗜 📞 🗑

Cambrai Lodge

Mr John Titchener

Oak Street, LECHLADE, GL7 3AY

T: 01367 253173 M: 07860 150467

🛏 2 £49.00 🛏 2 £49.00 (£39.00)

🛏 1 £67.00 🛏 2 £30.00 ⛹ ♿ 🖼 V 🐾

🚭 DRY ◆◆◆◆ 🏅 Victorian 4-poster bed available

Section 2

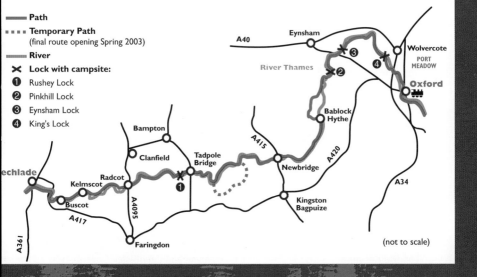

Lechlade to Oxford

This 50 km (31 miles) stretch is the most remote of the whole Trail. The Path follows the ever growing Thames as it slowly winds its way through the flat flood plain of the Thames Valley and you'll experience large skies and peaceful views. You'll rarely encounter settlements and will cross only a few, mostly minor, roads.

I f you want peace and quiet more than anything, then this is the section of the Thames Path for you to explore. Once you leave Lechlade behind, and have paid your respects to Old Father Thames at St John's Lock, you'll be hard-pressed to find many farmsteads or villages close to the Path until you reach the outskirts of Oxford. Luckily, however, your walk will be interspersed with the occasional road crossing with a welcoming pub on the river bank, and at one crossing a choice of pubs, one on each bank!

Mixed farming and lots of sky dominate the landscape here. You'll walk through meadows grazed by sheep or cattle, many with hedges abundant with blackberries as long as you're there at the right time of year. Other fields are planted with a variety of crops, their colour changing with the seasons and influencing the views you'll enjoy.

The river grows broader all the time, its course frequently marked by tall willows or the shorter alders, both liking to have their roots in water. Unfortunately alders are suffering from a fungal disease carried by water and in places are dying.

Not far from Lechlade you'll pass close to the small villages of Buscot and Kelmscot, and further on you should stop to look at the oldest bridge on the Thames at Radcot.

From Tenfoot Bridge to Shifford Lock the Path will be temporary until Spring 2003 following a rural route for about 3 km through Duxford. From then the Path will keep to the north bank before crossing to the south bank at Shifford Lock.

Maps

Landranger maps	163	Cheltenham and Cirencester
	164	Oxford
Explorer maps	170	Abingdon, Wantage and Vale of White Horse
	180	Oxford

Transport Information

| Rail Services | National Rail **T**: 08457 484950 or www.nationalrail.co.uk or www.railtrack.co.uk |
| Bus Services | National Public Transport Information Service **T**: 0870 608 2608 or www.pti.org.uk |

Taxi Services

Place	Name	Telephone numbers
Lechlade	CTs	01367 252575
Faringdon	Stephen Shaw	01367 240804
	Nigel Matson	01367 241121
	Doug Timms	01367 241820
	Shannon Cars	07855 173643 (mobile)
Southmoor	Southmoor Taxis	01865 820984
Oxford	City Taxis	01865 794000
	001 Taxis	01865 240000
	A.B.C. Taxis	01865 770077
	Ace Cars	01865 770000

Toilets at Locks

Radcot Lock
Rushey Lock, upstream of Tadpole Bridge
Eynsham Lock

Police

Gloucestershire	**T**: 01242 521 321
Oxfordshire	**T**: 01865 846000

Hospitals

Swindon	Princess Margaret Hospital, Okus Road, Swindon **T**: 01793 536231
Oxford	John Radcliffe Hospital, Headley Way, Headington, Oxford **T**: 01865 741166

Tourist Information Centres

All provide an accommodation booking service.

Place	Address/Opening Hours
Swindon	37 Regent Street, Swindon SN1 1JL **T**: 01793 530328 **F**: 01793 434031 **E**: infocentre@swindon.gov.uk www. visitswindon.co.uk **Opening hours:** All year: Mon-Sat 9:15-17:00
Faringdon	7a Market Place, Faringdon SN7 7HL **T/F**: 01367 242191 **Opening hours:** Summer (Apr 1-Oct 31): Mon-Fri 10:00-17:00; Sat 10:00-13:00 Winter (Nov 1-Mar 31): Mon-Sat 10:00-13:00
Witney	51a Market Square, Witney OX8 6AG **T**: 01993 775802 **F**: 01993 709261 **E**: cotswold@westoxon.gov.uk www.oxfordshirecotswolds.org **Opening hours:** Summer (Mar 1-Oct 31): Mon-Sat 9:30-17:30 Winter (Nov 1-Feb 28): Mon-Sat 10:00-16:30
Oxford	15-16 Broadstreet Oxford OX1 3AS **T**: 01865 726871 **F**: 01865 240261 **E**: tic@oxford.gov.uk; www.visitoxford.org **Opening hours:** Summer (Easter-Oct 31): Mon-Sat 9:00-17:00; Sun 10:00-15:30 Winter (Nov 1-Easter): Mon-Sat 9:30-17:00 Bank Holidays: 10:00-15:30

BUSCOT

SU2397 🥾 0.6km (0.4miles)

🚂 Swindon 18km (11.2miles) 📞

✉ | S M T W T F S | 🧺 | S M T W T F S |

🫖 | S M T W T F S |

☆ Buscot Park - National Trust
T: 01367 240786 www.buscot-park.com

Weston Farm   *closed Xmas, New Year*

Mrs Jean Woof
Buscot Wick, FARINGDON, SN7 8DJ
T: 01367 252222 **F:** 01367 252222
🛏 2 £50.00 🛏 1 £50.00 (£30.00)
👥 📺 V 🚭 DRY 🚗 🎣 ◆◆◆◆
🍴 ETC Silver Award

KELMSCOT

SU2599 🥾 0.5km (0.3miles)

🚂 Swindon 22.5km (14miles) 📞

🍺 | S M T W T F S | 🍴 | S M T W T F S |

☆ Kelmscott Manor. Limited opening times.
T: 01367 252486 www.kelmscottmanor.co.uk

The Plough at Kelmscot   *closed Mon*   INN

Mr M Platt
Kelmscot, LECHLADE, GL7 3HG
T: 01367 253543 **F:** 01367 252514
🛏 4 £70.00 (1 @ £60.00) 🛏 2 £70.00
(£45.00) 🛏 1 £85.00 🛏 1 £45.00 👥 ♿
📺 V 🏔 🚭 DRY 📷 💳 Visa, Mastercard,
American Express 🍴 ETC 3 Crowns Rating

The Plough at Kelmscot

Peacefully situated in an unspoiled village close to Kelmscott Manor and the Thames, the 17th century Plough is a favourite refreshment stop among the walking and boating fraternity.

T: 01367 253543

43

Portwell House Hotel

17th Century House in the centre of the ancient market town of Faringdon. Small family run hotel where you can be assured of a personal caring service and plenty of local knowledge. Good fresh home made food.

- Non-smokingthroughout.
- Group bookings welcome.

Phone Hugh & Denise Pakeman on 01367 240 197 for reservations

RADCOT

 SU2899 ⌂ on path

🚂 Swindon 24km (14.9miles)

🍺 |||||||||| ✗ ||||||||||
  S M T W T F S   S M T W T F S

FARINGDON

SU2895 ⌂ 4.5km (5.1miles)

🚂 Swindon 19.5km (12.2miles) ℹ

Town with full range of facilities,

www.faringdon.org for details of visitor attractions

☆ Faringdon Folly **T:** 01367 240 450

Portwell House Hotel Ⓗ

Mr & Mrs Hugh & Denise Pakeman
Market Place, FARINGDON, SN7 7HU
T: 01367 240197 **F:** 01367 244330
E: enquiries@portwellhouse.com
www.portwellhouse.com

🛏 3 £60.00 🛏 2 £60.00 (£45.00)
🛏 1 £75.00 🛏 2 £45.00 👫 (min age 2)
♿ 🖼 V 🔔 🚭 🅳🆁🆈 📷 🚗 🐾
Visa, Mastercard, Delta ◆◆◆

Camden House

Mrs Wynn Matson
28 Market Place, FARINGDON, SN7 7HU
T: 01367 241121 or 0845 458 2215
F: 01367 241999
🛏 1 £40.00 🛏 1 £40.00 (£25.00)
🛏 1 £45.00 🛏 2 £25.00 ⚥ ♿ V 🎿
DRY 🖶 🚗 ⚐

🏠 Sudbury House Hotel

Mr Andrew Ibbotson
Folly Hill, FARINGDON, SN7 8AA
T: 01367 241272 **F:** 01367 242346
E: stay@sudburyhouse.co.uk
www.sudburyhouse.co.uk
🛏 39 £65.00 🛏 10 £65.00 🛏 3
£85.00 ⚥ ♿ 🖥 V 🎿 🚭 DRY 🖶 ⚐ 💳
Visa, Mastercard, American Express, Delta
★★★

CLANFIELD

SP2801 🚶 2.9km (1.8miles)
🚌 Shipton, but Oxford offers best
rail & bus connect 16km (9.9miles) 📞

🍺	S	M	T	W	T	F	S	✕	S	M	T	W	T	F	S
✉	S	M	T	W	T	F	S	🧺	S	M	T	W	T	F	S

The Granary

Mrs Rosina Payne
Clanfield, BAMPTON, OX18 2SH
T: 01367 810266
🛏 1 £44.00 🛏 1 £44.00 🛏 1 £22.00
♿ V 🚭 DRY ◆◆◆

The Plough at Clanfield   *closed Xmas & New Year* 🏠

Mr John Hodges
Bourton Road, CLANFIELD, OX18 2RB
T: 01367 810222 **F:** 01367 810596
E: ploughatclanfield@hotmail.com
www.theploughatclanfield.com
🛏 10 £120.00 🛏 2 £120.00 (£90.00)
⚥ (min age 12) ♿ V 🎿 🚭 🚭 DRY 🖶
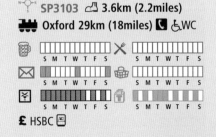
🚗 ⚐ 💳 Visa, Mastercard, American
Express, Delta, Diners ⬛ Awarded 3 stars
by AA

BAMPTON

SP3103 🚶 3.6km (2.2miles)
🚌 Oxford 29km (18miles) 📞 ♿WC

🍺	S	M	T	W	T	F	S	✕	S	M	T	W	T	F	S
✉	S	M	T	W	T	F	S	🧺	S	M	T	W	T	F	S
🗶	S	M	T	W	T	F	S	🗑	S	M	T	W	T	F	S

£ HSBC 🖶

Rushey Lock   *closed Nov - Mar*

The Lock Keeper
Tadpole Bridge, Buckland Marsh,
FARINGDON, SN7 8RF
T: 01367 870218
5

NEWBRIDGE

SP4001   on path
Oxford 18.5km (11.5miles)

S M T W T F S   S M T W T F S

TADPOLE BRIDGE

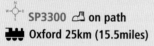

SP3300   on path
Oxford 25km (15.5miles)

S M T W T F S   S M T W T F S

BABLOCK HYTHE

SP4304   on path
Oxford 9.3km (5.8miles)

S M T W T F S   S M T W T F S

Newbridge

 The Ferryman Inn

Mr Peter Kelland
Bablock Hythe, NORTHMOOR, OX29 5AT
T: 01865 880028 **F:** 01865 880028
E: kelland@oxfree.com
www.smoothound.com/a12194.html

🛏 4 £55.00 🛏 2 £55.00 (£35.00)
🛏 2 £65.00 ♟ ♿ V 🔥 🚭 ⊘ DRY 🚴
⛺ £5.00 ♨ ♨ ♿WC 📞 CG
🍴 Breakfast £4.50/person extra

Spindle

EYNSHAM

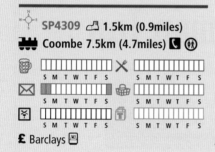

SP4309 🛏 1.5km (0.9miles)

🚂 Coombe 7.5km (4.7miles) 📞 ♿

🍺	S M T W T F S	🍴	S M T W T F S
✉	S M T W T F S	🧺	S M T W T F S
🎣	S M T W T F S	🗑	S M T W T F S

£ Barclays 🖃

⛺ Pinkhill Lock

The Lock Keeper
EYNSHAM, OX8 1JH
T: 01865 881452
⛺ 5 🔧 🚰 🚿 🚻 Limited facilities -
mens urinals only

⛺ Eynsham Lock

The Lock Keeper
Swinford Bridge, EYNSHAM, OX8 1BY
T: 01865 881324
⛺ 10 🔧 🚰 ♿

WOLVERCOTE

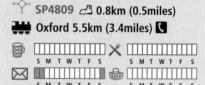

SP4809 🛏 0.8km (0.5miles)

🚂 Oxford 5.5km (3.4miles) 📞

| 🍺 | S M T W T F S | 🍴 | S M T W T F S |
| ✉ | S M T W T F S | 🧺 | S M T W T F S |

⛺ Kings Lock

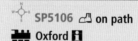

The Lock Keeper
Godstow Road, WOLVERCOTE, OX2 8PY
T: 01865 553403
⛺ 10 🔧 🚰 🚿 🚻 Limited facilities -
mens urinals only

OXFORD

SP5106 🛏 on path

🚂 Oxford 🛈

City with full range of services

Oxford has a wide range of accommodation; details can be obtained from the Tourist Information Centre. However, the accommodation providers below particularly welcome Thames Path walkers

www.visitoxford.org for details of the many visitor attractions

Sportsview Guest House

Mr & Mrs Mohinda Saini
106-110 Abingdon Road, OXFORD, OX1
4PX
T: 01865 244268 **M:** 07798 818190
F: 01865 249270
E: stay@sportsview-guest-
house.freeserve.co.uk
www.smoothound.com/a51941.html
4 £50.00 4 £50.00 (£45.00)
6 £69.00 6 £32.00 ♦♦ (min age 3) V ⊘
Visa, Mastercard, Delta, Switch & Solo
◆◆◆

Cornerways Guest House   *closed Xmas & New Year*

Mrs Carol Jeakings
282 Abingdon Road, OXFORD, OX1 4TA
T: 01865 240135 **F:** 01865 247652
E: jeakings@btinternet.com
1 £58.00 1 £58.00 (£45.00) 1
£70.00 1 £38.00 ♦♦ V ⊘ ◆◆◆

River Hotel   *closed Xmas & New Year*

Mrs P Jones
17 Botley Road, OXFORD, OX2 0AA
T: 01865 243475 **F:** 01865 724306
E: reception@riverhotel.co.uk
www.riverhotel.co.uk
9 £76.00 2 £86.00 (£70.00)
5 £96.00 4 £65.00 ♦♦ V DRY
Visa, Mastercard ◆◆◆

Oxford Youth Hostel

The Manager
2A Botley Road, OXFORD, OX2 0AB
T: 01865 762997 **F:** 01865 769402
E: oxford@yha.org.uk www.yha.org.uk
♦♦ ♿ ⊘ Visa, Mastercard, Delta
Dormitories: £19/adult, £14/child,
breakfast included

Brown's Guest House

Mr & Mrs G McHugh
281 Iffley Road, OXFORD, OX4 4AQ
T: 01865 246822 **F:** 01865 246822
E: brownsgh@hotmail.com
3 £60.00 2 £60.00 (£50.00)
4 £34.00 V ⊘ DRY Visa,
Mastercard, Delta ◆◆◆

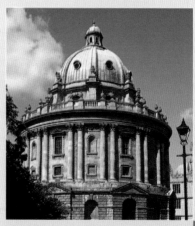

Radcliffe Camera, Oxford

YOUTH HOSTELS

yha

- Oxford
- Streatley
- Windsor
- Hampstead Heath
- Earl's Court
- Oxford Street
- Holland House
- City of London
- St Pancras
- Rotherhithe

Ten Youth Hostels lie along the Thames Path, seven are located in central London, with Oxford, Streatley and Windsor situated outside the capital. All offer a warm welcome and great value shared accommodation. However, if you prefer, most can also offer you a private room at little extra cost. You

Spires at Oxford

can really relax whilst enjoying a wide range of wholesome, tasy meals on offer. Other facilities you're likely to find include common room/television lounge, self-catering kitchen, laundry facilities and luggage store.

Stay at YHA Streatley and watch the boats at Goring-on-Thames. All the youth Hostels in London are ideally located for exploring the sites, but if you want to get away from the hustle and bustle, simply take a short underground ride to YHA Hampstead Heath where you'll find a quiet, countryside oasis.

YHA Hampstead Heath

The YHA is a membership organisation, offering a whole range of benefits to its members, including discounts at many popular attractions. You can join the YHA on arrival at the hostel or in advance before you visit by going on line at www.yha.org.uk or by contacting our friendly YHA Customer Services team T: 0870 770 8868

Section 3

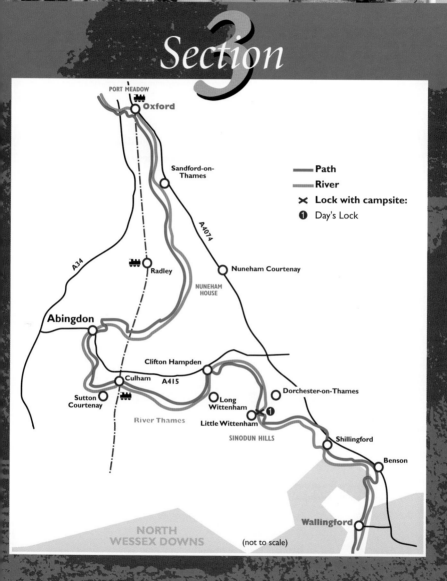

PORT MEADOW
Oxford

Sandford-on-Thames

A4074

Path
River
✕ **Lock with campsite:**
❶ **Day's Lock**

Radley

NUNEHAM
HOUSE

Nuneham Courtenay

A34

Abingdon

Clifton Hampden

Culham   A415

Sutton
Courtenay

Long
Wittenham

Dorchester-on-Thames

River Thames

Little Wittenham

SINODUN HILLS

Shillingford

Benson

NORTH
WESSEX DOWNS   (not to scale)

Wallingford

Oxford to Wallingford

Still essentially rural, this 38 km (24 miles) of the Thames Path is enhanced by the elegant city of Oxford and towns of Abingdon and Wallingford. As well as providing cultural diversions and refreshments, these are easy access points to the Path for those travelling by public transport.

3 A Taster

This section displays a variety of land use starting with the common land of Port Meadow in the northwest of Oxford, past the landscaped gardens of Nuneham House and onto views of the Sinodun Hills close to Dorchester with their distinctive clumps of trees and ancient Iron Age fort. Along with these you'll encounter modern farming of livestock and crops, the latter adding different colours to the landscape through the seasons, historic towns, attractive villages, and a marina at Benson a short distance before you reach Wallingford.

One of the best ways to arrive in Oxford is via the Thames Path from the north. If you decide not to explore this lovely city (although you are recommended to do so!) but to continue along the Path, you'll be amazed at the extent of green meadows and lack of urban intrusion. When you leave Oxford behind, with its historic buildings of Cotswold stone, you move into the clay belt where you'll find houses are mostly of brick construction.

This section includes seven locks owned and managed by the Environment Agency, all with tidy, colourful gardens and friendly lock keepers.

Maps

Landranger maps	164	Oxford
	175	Reading and Windsor
Explorer maps	170	Abingdon, Wantage and Vale of White Horse

Transport Information

Rail Services:	National Rail **T**: 08457 484950 or www.nationalrail.co.uk or www.railtrack.co.uk
Bus Services:	National Public Transport Information Service **T**: 0870 608 2608 or www.pti.org.uk

Taxi Services

Place	Name	Telephone numbers
Oxford	City Taxis	01865 794000
	001 Taxis	01865 240000
	A.B.C. Taxis	01865 770077
	Ace Cars	01865 770000
Radley	Rural Car Service	0800 074 3494
Abingdon	Auto Taxis	01235 527711
	Toots Taxis	01235 555599
	Phil's Taxis	01235 522555
	Vargan Taxis	01235 559606
Benson	A Cabs	01491 839982
	Pointings Taxis	01491 826679
Wallingford	Hills Taxis	01491 837022
	Rural Car Service	0800 074 3494

Toilets at Locks

Abingdon Lock
Culham Lock

Police

Oxfordshire   **T**: 01865 846000

Hospitals

Oxford   John Radcliffe Hospital, Headley Way, Headington, Oxford
               T: 01865 741166

Wallingford   Wallingford Community Hospital, Reading Road, Wallingford
                  T: 01491 698500

3   A Taster

Tourist Information Centres

All provide an accommodation booking service

Place	Address/Opening Hours
Oxford	15-16 Broadstreet, Oxford OX1 3AS **T**: 01865 726871 **F**: 01865 240261 **E**: tic@oxford.gov.uk www.visitoxford.org **Opening hours** Summer (Easter-Oct 31): Mon-Sat 9:00-17:00; Sun 10:00-15:30 Winter (Nov 1-Easter): Mon-Sat 9:30-17:00 Bank Holidays 10:00-15:30
Abingdon	25 Bridge Street, Abingdon OX14 3HN **T**: 01235 522711 **F**: 01235 535245 **Opening hours** Summer (Apr 1-Oct 31): Mon-Sat 10:00-17:00; Sun 13:30-16:15 Winter (Nov1-31 Mar): Mon-Fri 10:00-16:00; Sat 9:30-14:30
Wallingford	Town Hall, Market Place, Wallingford OX10 0EG **T**: 01491 826972 **F**: 01491 832925 **E**: ticwallingford@freenet.co.uk **Opening hours** All year: Mon-Sat 9:30-17:00

*The Barley Mow,
Clifton Hampden*

SANDFORD-ON-THAMES

SP5301 🥾 on path

🚂 Oxford 7.5km (4.7miles) 📞

🍺 [|||||||||||] ✕ [|||||||||||]
S M T W T F S   S M T W T F S

NUNEHAM COURTENAY

SU5599 🥾 3.5km (2.1miles)

🚂 Oxford 10.5km (6.5miles) 📞

Cross river at Sandford Lock or Clifton Hampden

🍺 [|||||||||||] ✕ [|||||||||||]
S M T W T F S   S M T W T F S
✉ [|||||||||||] 🧺 [|||||||||||]
S M T W T F S   S M T W T F S

☆ Harcourt Arboretum - oldest arboretum in the country, includes North American redwoods T: 01865 343501

The Old Bakery

Mrs Jill Addison

1/2 Nuneham Courtenay, OXFORD, OX44 9NX

T: 01865 343585 **F:** 01865 341336

E: addisonjill@hotmail.com

🛏 2 £65.00 🛏 1 £65.00 (£45.00) 👫

🐾 V 🏔 🚭 🚫 💳 Mastercard, Visa

RADLEY

SU5299 🥾 1.5km (0.9miles)

🚂 Radley 📞

🍺 [|||||||||||] ✕ [|||||||||||]
S M T W T F S   S M T W T F S
✉ [|||||||||||] 🧺 [|||||||||||]
S M T W T F S   S M T W T F S

3 Oxford to Wallingford

ABINGDON

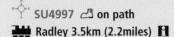

SU4997 on path
Radley 3.5km (2.2miles)

Large town with full range of services

Abingdon has a wide range of accommodation; details can be obtained from the Tourist Information Centre. However, the accommodation provider below particularly welcomes Thames Path walkers

☆ Abingdon Museum - winter open Tuesday - Sunday only 11am - 4pm. Telephone for details of lively exhibition programme **T:** 01235 523703

☆ Kingcraft Day Boats - The Bridge, Nags Head Island **T:** 01235 521125

☆ Abingdon Abbey **T:** 01235 525339

Kingfisher Barn Ltd

Miss Charlie Clement
Kingfisher Barn, Rye Farm, ABINGDON, OX14 3NN
T: 01235 537538 **F:** 01235 537538
E: info@kingfisherbarn.com
www.kingfisherbarn.com

 2 £49.50 8 £49.50 (£42.50)
Mastercard, Visa, American Express, Delta, Switch ★★★ Self-catering cottages: £290 per week

CULHAM

SU5095 on path
Culham 2.5km (1.6miles)

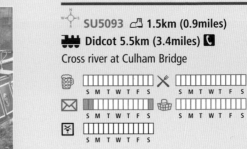

SUTTON COURTENAY

SU5093 1.5km (0.9miles)
Didcot 5.5km (3.4miles)
Cross river at Culham Bridge

56

Bekynton House   *closed Xmas*

Ms Susan Cornwall
7 The Green, SUTTON COURTENAY, OX14 4AE
T: 01235 848888 **M:** 07968 776691
F: 01235 848436 **E:** suecornwall@aol.com
🛏 1 £60.00 ⛵ 2 £60.00 (£30.00)
🛏 1 £30.00 ⚤ V ⊘ DRY ⊙ 👣
Self catering: £300/week for 2-bedroom
cottage

INN | The Fish

Mrs J Gaffney
4 Appleford Road, Sutton Courtenay,
ABINGDON, OX14 4NQ
T: 01235 848242 **F:** 01235 848014
www.thefish.uk.com
🛏 1 £50.00 ⛵ 1 £50.00 (£40.00)
🛏 1 £40.00 ⚤ V ⊘ ⊘ DRY 👣 💳
Visa, Mastercard, Delta, American Express
10% reduction if full dinner/lunch menu
is ordered

CLIFTON HAMPDEN

✛ SU5495 🛆 on path
🚂 Culham 1.8km (1.1miles) 📞

🍺	S M T W T F S	✕	S M T W T F S
📧	S M T W T F S	🧺	S M T W T F S
🗓	S M T W T F S		

Bridge House Caravan Site   *closed Nov – Mar* ⛺

Miss E Gower
Bridge House, Clifton Hampden,
ABINGDON, OX14 3EH
T: 01865 407725
⛺ 12 £5.00 🚐 25 £8.00 🔌 🚿 🚰 ♿
💡 DRY ⊙ CG

LONG WITTENHAM

✛ SU5493 🛆 2.5km (1.6miles)
🚂 Culham 3.8km (2.4miles) 📞
Cross river at Clifton Hampden Bridge

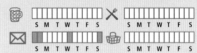

| 🍺 | S M T W T F S | ✕ | S M T W T F S |
| 📧 | S M T W T F S | 🧺 | S M T W T F S |

☆ Pendon Musuem of Miniature
Landscape and Transport - limited opening
T: 01865 407365
www.pendonmuseum.com

Witta's Ham Cottage   *closed Xmas*

Mrs Jill Mellor
High Street, Long Wittenham, ABINGDON,
OX14 4QH
T: 01865 407686 **F:** 01865 407469
E: martin.mellor@sjpp.co.uk
🛏 1 £50.00 ⛵ 1 £50.00 (£30.00)
🛏 1 £30.00 ⚤ (min age 10) 🔌 V 🔥 ⊘
🚗 ◆◆◆◆

Day's Lock and Thames Valley from Little Wittenham Clumps

Cottages at Clifton Hampden

3 Oxford to Wallingford

Little Wittenham

⊕ SU5693 🏠 0.5km (0.3miles)
🚂 Culham 5.5km (3.4miles) 📞
Cross river at Little Wittenham Bridge

☆ Little Wittenham Nature Reserve
T: 01865 407792
www.northmoortrust.co.uk

⛺ **Day's Lock** *closed Oct – Mar*

The Lock Keeper
Little Wittenham, ABINGDON, OX14 4RD
T: 01865 407768
⚊ 5 🔧 🔧 🔧 ⑪ 🗒

Dorchester-on-Thames

⊕ SU5794 🏠 2km (1.2miles)
🚂 Culham 6.5km (4miles) 📞 ♿WC

🍺	S	M	T	W	T	F	S	✕	S	M	T	W	T	F	S
✉	S	M	T	W	T	F	S	🧺	S	M	T	W	T	F	S
☕	S	M	T	W	T	F	S	🎌	S	M	T	W	T	F	S

☆ Dorchester Abbey & Museum
T: 01865 340007
www.dorchester-abbey.org.uk

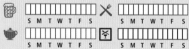
White Hart Hotel Ⓗ

Mr Sean Harris
High Street, DORCHESTER-ON-THAMES, OX10 7HN
T: 01865 340074 F: 01865 341082
E: whitehartdorch@aol.com
www.white-hart-hotel-dorchester.co.uk
🛏 16 £85.00 🛏 6 £85.00 (£75.00)
🛏 3 £120.00 🛏 2 £75.00 ♟ ♿ 📶 V
🐾 🚭 DRY VISA Mastercard, Visa, American Express, Delta ★★★ 🅜 Twin beds can be converted to double beds

Shillingford

⊕ SU5992 🏠 on path
🚂 Chosley 8.3km (5.2miles) 📞

| 🍺 | S | M | T | W | T | F | S | ✕ | S | M | T | W | T | F | S |
| ☕ | S | M | T | W | T | F | S | 🎌 | S | M | T | W | T | F | S |

⑈ The Kingfisher Inn

Mr Alexis Somarakis
27 Henley Road, SHILLINGFORD, OX10 7EL
T: 01865 858595
E: room@kingfisher-inn.co.uk
www.kingfisher-inn.co.uk
🛏 5 £72.50 🛏 1 £79.50 (£55.00) ♟
(min age 14) ♿ V 🐾 🚭 🚭 DRY 🚗 🅪
VISA Mastercard, Visa, American Express, Delta ◆◆◆◆

Marsh House

Mrs Patricia Nickson
7 Court Drive, Shillingford, WALLINGFORD, OX10 7ER
T: 01865 858496 **M:** 07702 454837
F: 01865 858496
E: marsh.house@talk21.com
🛏 1 £50.00 🛏 1 £50.00 (£30.00)
🛏 1 £25.00 ♀♂ (min age 8) V 🚭 DRY
🥾 ◆◆◆

North Farm   *closed Xmas & New Year*

Mrs Hilary Warburton
Shillingford Hill, WALLINGFORD, OX10 8NB
T: 01865 858406 **F:** 01865 858519
E: northfarm@compuserve.com
www.country-accom.co.uk/north-farm
🛏 2 £53.00 🛏 1 £53.00 (£38.00) ♀♂
(min age 8) 📺 V ⚠🚭 DRY 🚗
◆◆◆◆ 🅷 ETC Silver Award

Blackberries

BENSON

🧭 SU6191 🏕 on path
🚂 Cholsey 8.2km (5.1miles) 📞 ♿

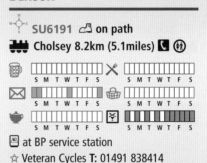

📱 at BP service station
☆ Veteran Cycles **T:** 01491 838414
By appointment only

Brookside   *closed Xmas & New Year*

Mrs Jill Folley
Brook Street, BENSON, OX10 6LJ
T: 01491 838289 **M:** 07979 813302
F: 01491 838289
🛏 1 £50.00 (£40.00) 🛏 1 £75.00
♀♂ 📺 V DRY 🚗 🥾 ◆◆◆
🅷 En-suite rooms

2 Castle Close

Mrs Janet Fletcher
Benson, WALLINGFORD, OX10 6SN
T: 01491 835505 **M:** 07990 517324
🛏 1 £50.00 🛏 1 £35.00 V DRY
🚗🥾

3   Oxford to Wallingford

WALLINGFORD

SU6089 ⌂ on path
🚂 Cholsey 4.7km (2.9miles) 🛈

Town with full range of facilities,

www.wallingford.co.uk for details of visitor attractions

Wallingford has a wide range of accommodation; details can be obtained from the Tourist Information Centre. However, the accommodation providers below particularly welcome Thames Path walkers

☆ Wallingford Museum **T:** 01491 835065

🏨 The George Hotel

Mr Oliver Round-Turner
High Street, WALLINGFORD, OX10 0BS
T: 01491 836665 **F:** 01491 825359
E: info@george-hotel-wallingford.com
www.peelhotel.com
🛏 20 £78.00 🛏 9 £78.00 (£58.00)
🛏 1 £100.00 🛏 9 £48.00 ⚤ ♿ V ♺
🚭 DRY 📺 🐕 💳 Visa, Mastercard,
American Express, Delta, Switch ★★★
🅷 Smoking is not allowed in some rooms

The Studio

Mrs Pamela Smith
85 Wantage Road, WALLINGFORD, OX10 0LT
T: 01491 837277 **E:** pam@prufit.co.uk
www.wallingfordbandb.co.uk
🛏 1 £50.00 🛏 1 £50.00 (£35.00)
🛏 1 £25.00 ⚤ (min age 4) 🐕 V 🚭 DRY
📺 🚗 🐕

52 Blackstone Road

Mrs Enid Barnard
WALLINGFORD, OX10 8JL
T: 01491 201917
E: enid.barnard@ebarnard.fsnet.co.uk
🛏 1 £35.00 (£23.00) 🛏 1 £17.50
V 🚭 DRY

Little Gables

Jill & Tony Reeves
166 Crowmarsh Hill, WALLINGFORD, OX10 8BG
T: 01491 837834 **M:** 07860 148882
F: 01491 834426 **E:** jill@stayingaway.com
www.stayingaway.com
🛏 3 £55.00 (£40.00) ⚤ ♿ V ♺ 🚭
DRY 🐕 ◆◆◆ 🅷 Twin beds can be converted to double beds; family room available from £75

Section 4

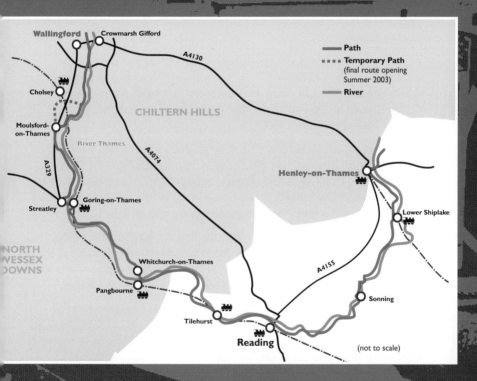

Wallingford to Henley-on-Thames

A 44 km (27 miles) stretch of the Path alongside the Thames during an especially serene stage as it enters the Chiltern Hills which provide a wonderful wooded backdrop. You'll regularly find settlements ranging in size from villages to the large town of Reading many of which provide good public transport access to the Path and refreshments.

4 A Taster

The first few kilometres of your walk from Wallingford pass through very open countryside with large undulating arable fields stretching away to the east to a beech wood skyline. Soon, however, you reach the Goring Gap with the Berkshire Downs rising on one side and the Chiltern Hills on the other. This is the narrowest part of the Thames Valley and the hills to either side seem almost like mountains compared to the flatness of the Oxfordshire clay vale through which the river has recently flowed.

At the twin settlements of Streatley and Goring the Thames Path is crossed by another of England's 13 National Trails, The Ridgeway. This ancient route enters the Goring Gap from the chalk downs to the west and then heads northeast along the Chilterns escarpment having followed the Thames for a few kilometres on the opposite bank to the Thames Path.

Between Goring and Mapledurham the Path, its river, the railway and main road all squeeze together between chalk hills clad with the trees which give the Chiltern Hills its character. Your approach to Reading through Purley is currently a temporary one whilst a hopefully less urban route can be found, but the Path through Reading itself is surprisingly pleasant for it passes through the least urbanised area.

From Reading to Sonning cyclists can share the Path, but from Sonning, with its lovely 18th century hump-backed bridge, the Path narrows and is for walkers only. As you walk towards Henley, famous for its Royal Regatta, you'll enjoy a landscape of gentle wooded hills, fine houses, and, of course, the ever widening Thames.

There are a few places where the route of the Path is still temporary whilst the lengthy legal and construction work to create new footpaths is completed. These are at Moulsford (new route opening in summer 2003), Purley and Shiplake. However, it is hoped that this work will be finished soon.

Maps

Landranger maps	175	Reading and Windsor
	174	Newbury and Wantage
Explorer maps	170	Abingdon, Wantage and Vale of White Horse
	171	Chiltern Hills West

Transport Information

Rail Services:	National Rail **T**: 08457 484950 or www.nationalrail.co.uk or www.railtrack.co.uk
Bus Services:	National Public Transport Information Service **T**: 0870 608 2608 or www.pti.org.uk

Taxi Services

Place	Name	Telephone numbers
Wallingford	Hills Taxis	01491 837022
	Rural Car Service	0800 074 3494
Goring	Golden Taxis	01491 871111
	Murdocks Taxis	01491 872029
Reading	Theale Taxis	0118 9302345
	Thames Valley Taxis Ltd	0118 9484848
	Just Cars	0118 9500400
	Premier Cars	0118 9500500
Sonning	Woodley	0800 654 321
	Top Cars	0118 9442222
Henley	Chiltern Taxis	01491 578899
	County Cars	01491 579696
	Harris Taxis	01491 577036
	Talbot Taxis	01491 574222

Toilets at Locks

Cleeve Lock, upstream of Goring-on-Thames

Shiplake Lock

Police

Oxfordshire and Berkshire   **T**: 01865 846000

Hospitals

Wallingford	Wallingford Community Hospital, Reading Road, Wallingford **T:** 01491 698500
Reading	The Royal Berkshire Hospital, London Road, Reading **T:** 0118 9875111
Henley	Townlands Hospital, York Road, Henley **T:** 01491 572544 (Minor injuries only)

Tourist Information Centres

All provide an accommodation booking service

Place	Address/Opening Hours
Wallingford	Town Hall, Market Place, Wallingford OX10 0EG **T:** 01491 826972 **F:** 01491 832925 **E:** ticwallingford@freenet.co.uk **Opening hours:** All year: Mon-Sat 9:30-17:00
Reading	Reading Visitor Centre, Church Lane, Chain St Reading RG1 2HX **T:** 0118 956 6226 **F:** 0118 939 9885 **E:** touristinfo@reading.gov.uk www.readingtourism.org.uk **Opening hours:** All year: Mon-Fri 9:30-17:00, Sat 9:30-16:00
Henley-on-Thames	King's Arms Barn, Kings Road, Henley-on-Thames RG9 2DG **T:** 01491 578034 **F:** 01491 411766 **E:** henleytic@hotmail.com **Opening hours:** Summer: Mon-Sat 9:30-18:00, Sun 10:00-17:00 Winter: Mon-Sat 9:30-17.00, Sun 10:00-16:00

CROWMARSH GIFFORD

SU6189 🥾 0.5km (0.3miles)

🚂 Cholsey 5.7km (3.5miles) 📞

🍺								✕							
	S	M	T	W	T	F	S		S	M	T	W	T	F	S
✉								🧺							
	S	M	T	W	T	F	S		S	M	T	W	T	F	S
✇								🗑							
	S	M	T	W	T	F	S		S	M	T	W	T	F	S

⛺ Riverside Park *Apr-Oct*

Mr Jeremy Mayo
The Street, Crowmarsh Gifford,
WALLINGFORD, OX10 8EB
T: 01491 835232 / 839755
F: 01491 835232
⛺ 🚐 27 £7.00 🚿 🚿 🚰 ♿ 📋 📞
🍴 Plus 75p/adult

⛺ Bridge Villa Caravan & Camp Site *closed Jan*

Mr E L Townsend
Bridge Villa, The Street, Crowmarsh
Gifford, WALLINGFORD, OX10 6MR
T: 01491 836860 M: 07710 452429
F: 01491 839103
E: ael.townsend@btinternet.com
⛺ 111 £7.00 🚐 111 £8.00 🚿 🚿 🚰
♿WC 📋 📞 🎱 CG 💳 Visa, Mastercard,
Delta

CHOLSEY

SU5886 🥾 1.5km (0.9miles)

🚂 Cholsey 📞

🍺								✕							
	S	M	T	W	T	F	S		S	M	T	W	T	F	S
✉								🧺							
	S	M	T	W	T	F	S		S	M	T	W	T	F	S
✇															
	S	M	T	W	T	F	S								

£ Abbey National 🏧

MOULSFORD-ON-THAMES

SU5983 🥾 on path

🚂 Cholsey 3.4km (2.1miles) 📞

🍺								✕							
	S	M	T	W	T	F	S		S	M	T	W	T	F	S
✇															
	S	M	T	W	T	F	S								

White House *closed Xmas & New Year*

Mrs Maria Watsham
Moulsford-on-Thames, WALLINGFORD,
OX10 9JD
T: 01491 651397 M: 07831 372243
F: 01491 652560
E: mwatsham@hotmail.com
🛏 1 £50.00 🛏 1 £50.00 (£35.00)
🛏 1 £30.00 ✳ V 🚭 🚫 🚭 DRY 📺 🚗
🚶 ◆◆◆◆ 🍴 ETC Silver Award;
evening meals must be booked in advance

4 Wallingford to Henley-on-Thames

STREATLEY

 SU5980 ⌂ **on path**

🚂 **Goring and Streatly 1.2km (0.7miles)** 📞

S M T W T F S   S M T W T F S

☆ Basildon Park - National Trust property about 3km south of Streatley
T: 01494 755558 www.nationaltrust.org.uk

Streatley Youth Hostel *closed Jan and weekdays Dec & Feb*

Mr Nick Crivich
Reading Road, Streatley, READING, RG8 9JJ
T: 01491 872278 **F:** 01491 873056
E: streatley@yha.org.uk www.yha.org.uk
🛏 1 £34.00 ⋔ V 🈲 🚭 🚫 DRY 💳
Visa, Mastercard, American Express, Delta
★🄗 Dormitory accommodation: £11.50/adult

Stable Cottages

Mrs Diana Fenton
Streatley, READING, RG8 9JX
T: 01491 874408
E: dianam@freenetname.co.uk
🛏 1 £46.00 (£23.00) 🛏 1 £23.00 ⋔ (min age 8) 🖼 V 🈲 🚭 DRY 🅟 🚗 🐾

Pennyfield *closed Xmas & New Year*

Mrs Maureen Vanstone
The Coombe, STREATLEY, RG8 9QT
T: 01491 872048 **M:** 07774 946182
F: 01491 872048
E: mandrvanstone@hotmail.com
www.pennyfield.co.uk
🛏 2 £55.00 🛏 1 £55.00 (£55.00)
⋔ (min age 11) V 🈲 🚭 DRY 🅟 🚗 🐾
◆◆◆◆ 🄗 ETC Silver Award; all rooms en-suite

GORING-ON-THAMES

 SU6081 ⌂ **on path**

🚂 **Goring and Streatley**

Small town with full range of services

www.goring-gap.co.uk for details of visitor attractions

£ HSBC 🏧, Lloyds TSB

Northview House *closed Xmas & New Year*

Mrs I Sheppard
Farm Road, Goring-on-Thames, READING, RG8 0AA
T: 01491 872184
E: hi@goring-on-thames.freeserve.co.uk
🛏 2 £40.00 🛏 1 £40.00 ⋔ 🖼 V 🈲 🚭 DRY 🅟 🐾

 Miller of Mansfield

Mr Martin Williamson
High Street, Goring-on-Thames, READING,
RG8 9AW
T: 01491 872829 **F:** 01491 874200
www.millerofmansfield.co.uk

4 £65.00   4 £65.00 (£49.50)
1 £75.00   1 £49.50 ✦✦✦

DRY Mastercard, Visa ◆◆◆

WHITCHURCH-ON-THAMES

SU6377 on path
Pangbourne 1km (0.6miles)

S M T W T F S   S M T W T F S

Goring-on-Thames Lock

4 Wallingford to Henley-on-Thames

PANGBOURNE

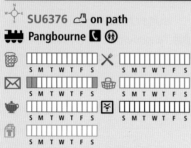

SU6376 ⌂ on path

🚂 Pangbourne 📞 ♿

£ NatWest 🖃, Lloyds TSB, Barclays
☆ Beale Park - wildlife park set in 400
acres on the banks of the Thames.
T: 01189 845172 www.bealepark.co.uk

TILEHURST

SU6674 ⌂ on path

🚂 Tilehurst 📞

£ Lloyds TSB 🖃, Barclays 🖃, NatWest 🖃,
HSBC 🖃

Warren Dene Hotel 🏨

Mr Alan Jardine
1017 Oxford Road, Tilehurst, READING,
RG31 6TL
T: 0118 9422556 **F:** 0118 9451096
E: wdh@globalnet.co.uk
www.warendenehotel.com

🛏 2 £48.00 🛏 2 £48.00 (£40.00)
🛏 3 £60.00 🛏 1 £32.00 � V 🚭
◆◆◆◆ 🅿 Transport can be arranged
through local taxi firm

READING

SU7173 ⌂ on path

🚂 Reading ℹ

Large town with full range of services.

*Reading has a wide range of
accommodation; details can be
obtained from the Tourist Information
Centre.*
www.readingtourism.org.uk for details of
the many visitor attractions

SONNING

 SU7675 🥾 on path

🚂 Twyford 4.5km (2.8miles) 📞

🍺	S M T W T F S	✕	S M T W T F S
✉	S M T W T F S	🧺	S M T W T F S
☕	S M T W T F S	🎣	S M T W T F S

LOWER SHIPLAKE

 SU7678 🥾 on path

🚂 Shiplake 2km (1.2miles) 📞

🍺	S M T W T F S	✕	S M T W T F S
✉	S M T W T F S	🧺	S M T W T F S
☕	S M T W T F S		

Sonning Bridge

4 Wallingford to Henley-on-Thames

HENLEY-ON-THAMES

 SU7682 ⌂ on path

🚂 Henley-on-Thames ⊞

Town with full range of services

Henley has a wide range of accommodation; details can be obtained from the Tourist Information Centre. However, the accommodation providers below particularly welcome Thames Path walkers

☆ River and Rowing Museum **T:** 01491 415600 www.rrm.co.uk

Coldharbour House   *closed Dec & Jan*

Mrs Diana Jones
3 Coldharbour Close, HENLEY-ON-THAMES, RG9 1QF
T: 01491 575229 **F:** 01491 575229
E: coldharbourhouse@aol.com
🛏 1 £60.00 🛏 1 £55.00 (£40.00) 🛏 1 £30.00 ♟ (min age 5) 📺 V ⊗ DRY 🚗 ◆◆◆◆

Five New Street

Mrs Carole Hill
5 New Street, HENLEY-ON-THAMES, RG9 2BP
T: 01491 411711 **M:** 07973 566679
E: fivenewstreet@aol.com
www.ccflights.com/henley
🛏 2 £50.00 🛏 1 £75.00 ♟ (min age 12) V ⊗ DRY 💳 Visa, Mastercard, Delta

---

Lenwade   *closed Xmas & New Year*

Mrs J Williams
3 Western Road, HENLEY-ON-THAMES, RG9 1JL
T: 01491 573468 **F:** 01491 573468
E: lenwadeuk@aol.com
www.w3b-ink.com/lenwade
🛏 2 £60.00 🛏 1 £60.00 (£45.00) ♟ V ⊗ DRY ◆◆◆◆◆

Abbottsleigh

Mrs K Bridekirk
107 St Mark's Road, HENLEY-ON-THAMES RG9 1LP
T: 01491 572982 **M:** 07958 424337
F: 01491 572982
🛏 1 £60.00 🛏 1 £60.00 (£40.00) 🛏 1 £40.00 ♟ V ⊗ DRY 🚗 ◆◆◆
⛺ En-suite rooms available. Self catering, sleeping 3, £60.00 per night

Section 5

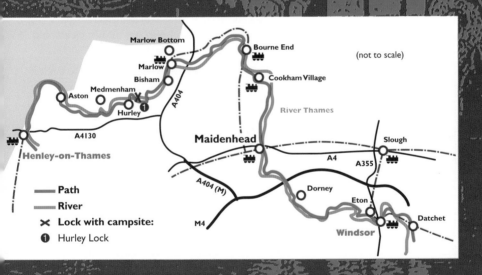

Marlow Bottom

Bourne End

(not to scale)

Marlow

Bisham

Cookham Village

Medmenham

Aston

River Thames

Hurley

❶

Maidenhead

A404

A4130

Slough

A4

A355

Henley-on-Thames

A404 (M)

Dorney

Eton

Datchet

M4

Windsor

━━ **Path**

━━ **River**

✕ **Lock with campsite:**

❶ Hurley Lock

Henley-on-Thames to Windsor

The pleasures of this 37 km (23 miles) stretch of the Path lie in the combination of walking beside the now mature river surrounded by the wooded slopes of the Chiltern Hills and the opportunity of exploring numerous pretty villages and towns, all with historical associations with famous people. As well, this section is very easily reached by public transport.

5 A Taster

Leaving Henley you follow the whole length of the Royal Regatta rowing course through increasingly rural grass meadows to Temple Island the starting point for the races. The small temple is in fact a fishing lodge built as a landscape feature to enhance the view from nearby Fawley Court. Indeed, along the whole route to Windsor you'll come across many fine houses with landscaped gardens or parks, now owned, one imagines, by the rich and famous of today.

Before you reach the attractive town of Marlow the Path does usually become busier. You'll also have passed Hurley and Bisham, both with tremendous stories from the past and fine buildings to see. Marlow, like Henley, has its own regatta and is arguably set in the most beautiful stretch of the Thames Valley.

Onto Cookham, where renowned artist Stanley Spencer lived, and beyond to a reach of the river set between towering trees, magnificent during autumn, above which you'll catch a glimpse of Cliveden House. This gained a colourful reputation for political intrigue both in the 1930s and later in the 1960s when the Profumo affair hit the headlines as a result of 'activities' in one of the riverside cottages you'll see on the far bank.

Maidenhead is prettily suburban having developed during the Edwardian era when the river here, and town, was packed with day trippers from London. From here the river becomes more commercial, the population pressure increases and the banks become lined with houses, many of them grand. Views of Windsor Castle are visible for many miles high on the last chalky outcrop of the Chilterns.

Temple Island, downstream of Henley

Maps

Landranger maps	175	Reading and Windsor
Explorer maps	171	Chiltern Hills West
	172	Chiltern Hills East
	160	Windsor, Weybridge and Bracknell

Transport Information

Rail Services:	National Rail **T**: 08457 484950 or www.nationalrail.co.uk or www.railtrack.co.uk
Bus Services:	National Public Transport Information Service **T**: 0870 608 2608 or www.pti.org.uk

Taxi Services

Place	Name	Telephone numbers
Henley	Chiltern Taxis	01491 578899
	County Cars	01491 579696
	Harris Taxis	01491 577036
	Talbot Taxis	01491 574222
Marlow	Bertran's	01628 485573
	Marlow Cars	01628 476395
Bourne End	Bourne End Cars	01628 523232
	Prestige Executive Cars	01628 533111
Maidenhead	A - Z Cars	01628 621234
	Embassy Cars	01628 780052
	Best Way Taxis	01628 485573
	Station Taxis	01628 771000
Windsor	Executive Cars of Windsor	01753 833500
	Five Star Car Hire	01753 859555
	Siverline of Windsor	01753 880765
	Windsor Radio Cars	01753 677677

5 A Taster

Toilets at Locks

Hurley Lock

Temple Lock, 1km downstream of Hurley

Marlow Lock

Cookham Lock

Bray Lock

Boveney Lock, southwest of the village of Eton Wick

Romney Lock, 1/2 km downstream of Windsor

Old Windsor Lock

Police

Berkshire & Buckinghamshire   **T**: 01865 846000

Hospitals

Henley   Townlands Hospital, York Road, Henley
                         T: 01491 572544 (Minor injuries only)

High Wycombe   Wycombe General Hospital, Queen Alexandra Road, High Wycombe
                         T: 01494 526161

Bisham Church

Tourist Information Centres

All provide an accommodation booking service.

Place	Address/Opening Hours
Henley-on-Thames	King's Arms Barn, Kings Road, Henley-on-Thames RG9 2DG **T**: 01491 578034 **F**: 01491 411766 **E**: henleytic@hotmail.com **Opening hours**: Summer: Mon-Sat 9:30-18:00, Sun 10:00-17:00 Winter: Mon-Sat 9:30-17.00, Sun 10:00-16:00
Marlow	31 High Street, Marlow SL7 1AU **T**: 01628 483597 **F**: 01628 471915 **E**: tourism_enquiries@wycombe.gov.uk **Opening hours**: Summer (Easter-Sep 30): Mon-Fri 9:00-17:00; Sat 9.30-17:00 Winter (Oct 1-Easter): Mon-Fri 9:00-17:00; Sat 9:30-16.00
Maidenhead	The Library, St Ives Road, Maidenhead SL6 1QU **T**: 01628 796502 **F**: 01628 781110 Accommodation hotline: 01628 781110 **E**: maidenhead.tic@rbwm.gov.uk www.maidenhead.gov.uk **Opening hours**: All year: Mon-Fri 9:30-17:00 Sat 9:30-16:00
Windsor	24 High Street, Windsor SL4 1LH **T**: 01753 743900 (general information) **T**: 01753 743907 (accommodation bookings) **F**: 01753 743904 **E**: windsor.tic@rbwm.gov.uk www. windsor.gov.uk **Opening hours**: Summer (Apr-Sep): Mon-Sun 10:00-17:00 Winter (Oct-Mar): Mon-Sun 10:00-16:00

5 Henley-on-Thames to Windsor

ASTON

SU7884 on path

Henley-on-Thames 4.5km (2.8miles)

MEDMENHAM

SU8084 3km (1.9miles)

Henley-on-Thames 7.5km (4.7miles) ☎

Cross river at Hambleden Lock

[INN] Ye Olde Dog & Badger

Mr Michael Bridges
Henley Road, MEDMENHAM, SL7 2HE
T: 01491 571362
E: michaelbridges@hotmail.com

2 £55.00 1 £55.00 ♥♥ ◻ V ⚠

🚫 ⊘ DRY VISA Visa, Mastercard, American Express, Delta

HURLEY

SU8283  on path

Marlow 6km (3.7miles) ☎

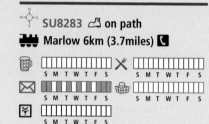

Hurley Lock   *closed Oct – Mar*

The Lockkeeper
Mill Lane, Hurley, MAIDENHEAD, SL6 1SA
T: 01628 824334

△ 10 🔧 🚿 🚾 ♿ ▯

MARLOW

SU8586 on path

Marlow 🅷

Town with full range of services

Marlow has a wide range of accommodation; details can be obtained from the Tourist Information Centre. However, the accommodation providers below particularly welcome Thames Path walkers

Longridge Scout Boating Centre *closed Nov - Mar*

Mr G Bucknell
Quarry Wood Road, MARLOW, SL7 1RE
T: 01628 483252 **F:** 01628 483252
E: admin@longridge.org.uk
www.longridge.org.uk
🏕 20 £3.90 🚰 🚰 ♿WC 📋 📞
Youth groups only - book in advance

8 Firview Close

Mrs P E King
MARLOW, SL7 1SZ
T: 01628 485735
🛏 1 £50.00 🛏 1 £50.00 (£36.00) 👫
V 🚭 DRY 📟

Glade End Guest House

Mrs Susan Peperell
2 Little Marlow Road, MARLOW, SL7 1HD
T: 01628 471334 **M:** 07774 107445
F: 01628 478154 **E:** sue@gladeend.com
www.gladeend.com
🛏 3 £75.00 🛏 3 £75.00 (£75.00)
🛏 1 £45.00 👫 (min age 5) ♿ V 🚭
DRY 📟 Mastercard, Visa, Delta,
American Express ◆◆◆◆

18 Rookery Court

Mrs Gill Bullen
MARLOW, SL7 3HR
T: 01628 486451 **M:** 07970 555814
E: gillbullen@compuserve.com
🛏 1 £50.00 (£35.00) ♿ V 🚭 DRY
📟 🚗 ◆◆◆◆ ETC Silver
Award; en-suite room

Hambleden Lock

MARLOW BOTTOM

SU8488 🏕 3km (1.9miles)

🚂 Marlow 3.5km (2.2miles) 📞

S M T W T F S   ✕   S M T W T F S
✉   S M T W T F S   🧺   S M T W T F S

Acorn Lodge

Mrs Peggy Peers-Johnson
79 Marlow Bottom Road, MARLOW, SL7 3NA
T: 01628 472197 **M:** 07718 757601
F: 01628 487450 **E:** davidpj@freenet.co.uk
🛏 3 £59.00 🛏 1 £59.00 **(£40.00)**
🛏 1 £75.00 🛏 4 £37.50 👫 (min age 5)
V 🚭 DRY ◻ 🚗 🐾 VISA Visa,
Mastercard, American Express, Delta ◆◆◆
⛺ Self-catering: £45/night, min. 2 nights

BOURNE END

SU8987 🏕 on path

🚂 Bourne End 📞 ♿

S M T W T F S   ✕   S M T W T F S
✉   S M T W T F S   🧺   S M T W T F S
☕   S M T W T F S   🎿   S M T W T F S
🍵   S M T W T F S

£ NatWest 🏧, Lloyds TSB 🏧, Barclays 🏧

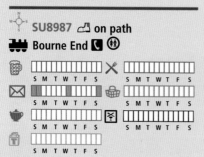

COOKHAM VILLAGE

SU8985 ⛺ on path

🚉 Cookham Rise 1.6km (1miles) 📞 ♿

☆ Stanley Spencer Gallery T: 01628 471885
www.stanleyspencer.org.uk

MAIDENHEAD

SU8981 ⛺ on path

🚉 Maidenhead Central ℹ

Large town with full range of services

Maidenhead has a wide range of accommodation; details can be obtained from the Tourist Information Centre. However, the accommodation providers below particularly welcome Thames Path walkers

☆ Cliveden National Trust property about 2 km upstream of Maidenhead overlooking the Thames T: 01494 755562
www.nationaltrust.org.uk

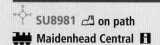
Ray Corner Guest House *closed Xmas*

Mr Graham Steptoe
141 Bridge Road, MAIDENHEAD, SL6 8NQ
T: 01628 632784 **M:** 07866 972242
F: 01628 783924
E: info@raycorner.fsnet.co.uk
www.raycorner.fsnet.co.uk
🛏 2 £50.00 🛏 1 £60.00 (£47.00) 🛏
2 £65.00 🛏 1 £47.00 ⛄ ♿ V 🚭 ◆◆◆

Copperfields Guest House *closed Xmas & New Year*

Mrs Joy Lindsay
54 Bath Road, MAIDENHEAD, SL6 4JY
T: 01628 674941
🛏 1 £60.00 🛏 2 £60.00 (£50.00)
🛏 5 £40.00 ⛄ (min age 10) 🐾 🚭

Hawthorn

DORNEY

 SU9379 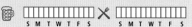 **1.5km (0.9miles)**

🚂 **Windsor & Eton Riverside 5.5km (3.4miles)** 📞

🍺 |||||||||||| ✕ ||||||||||||
   S M T W T F S   S M T W T F S

☆ Dorney Court **T:** 01628 604638
www.dorneycourt.co.uk

☆ Jubilee river flood alleviation scheme with recreational opportunities
www.environment-agency.gov.uk

Amerden Caravan & Camping Park   *Apr-Oct* ⛺

Mrs B Hakesley
Old Marsh Lane, Dorney Reach,
MAIDENHEAD, SL6 0EE
T: 01628 627461 **F:** 01628 627461
⛺ 25 £6.00 🚐 25 £10.00 🚰 🚿 🚿
♿WC 🏧 🖨 📞 🎲 CG ★★★★
🏠 100m from Path. Self catering available, £240/week

*Cliveden Estate
north of Medmenham*

ETON

⌖ SU9677 ◿ on path
🚋 Windsor & Eton Riverside 0.5km
(0.3miles) 📞 ♿WC

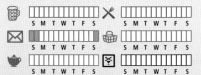

🍺 | S M T W T F S | ✕ | S M T W T F S |
📧 | S M T W T F S | 🧺 | S M T W T F S |
🫖 | S M T W T F S | ⌧ | S M T W T F S |

£ Barclays 🏧, Coutts 🏧

WINDSOR

⌖ SU9676 ◿ on path
🚋 Windsor Central 🅷

Town with full range of services

Windsor has a wide range of accommodation; details can be obtained from the Tourist Information Centre. However, the accommodation providers below particularly welcome Thames Path walkers

☆ Windsor Castle **T:** 01753 831118
www.royalresidences.com

☆ LEGOLAND® Windsor **T:** 08705 040404
www.legoland.co.uk

☆ Savill Garden **T:** 01753 847518
www.savillgarden.co.uk

Langton House   *closed Xmas & New Year*

Mr Paul Fogg
46 Alma Road, WINDSOR, SL4 3HA
T: 01753 858299 **F:** 01753 858299
E: paulbfogg@langtonhouse.com
www.langtonhouse.com
🛏 2 £73.00 🛏 1 £73.00 (£60.00)
🛏 1 £83.00 ⚤ V 🚭 DRY ◆◆◆◆

The Carriage House

Mrs D Airey
12 Osborne Mews, WINDSOR, SL4 3DE
T: 01753 855062
E: carriagehouse12@hotmail.com
🛏 1 £55.00 🛏 1 £55.00 (£45.00) ⚤
(min age 10) V 🚭 DRY

Clarence Hotel

Mr A Lalani
9 Clarence Road, WINDSOR, SL4 5AE
T: 01753 864436 **F:** 01753 857060
www.clarence-hotel.co.uk
🛏 5 £67.00 🛏 6 £67.00 (£61.00)
🛏 5 £76.00 🛏 4 £55.00 ⚤ 🐕 V DRY
📷 VISA Mastercard, Visa, American
Express, Delta ◆◆

The Laurels

Mrs Lillian Joyce
22 Dedworth Road, WINDSOR, SL4 5AY
T: 01753 855821
1 £45.00 (£25.00) 1 £25.00 V
DRY

Humes

Mrs Mabel Hume
2 Benning Close, WINDSOR, SL4 4YS
T: 01753 852294
1 £45.00 (£30.00) 1 £65.00
(min age 3) V

Windsor Youth Hostel *closed Xmas & New year*

The Manager
Edgeworth House, Mill Lane, WINDSOR,
SL4 5JE
T: 01753 861710 **F:** 01753 832100
E: winsdor@yha.org.uk
www.yha.org.uk
DRY Visa, Mastercard, American
Express, Delta Dormitories:
£11.50/adult, £8.25/child, no breakfast.
NB. This hostel may close during 2003,
please enquire

~ *Humes* ~

A modern detached house situated in a quiet residential area 2
miles from Windsor town centre, castle and Legoland.

Tel 01753 852294

Section 6

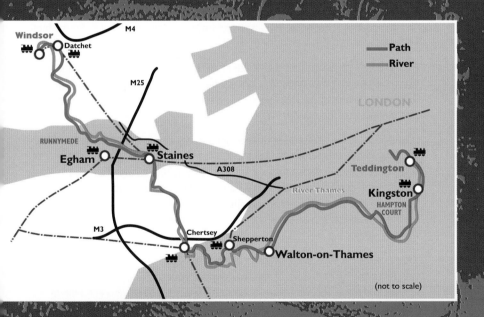

Windsor to Teddington

This last non-tidal 39 km (24 miles) of the Thames Path follows a truly Royal Thames from Windsor Castle to beyond Hampton Court with much of interest in between, including Runnymede where the Magna Carta was signed in 1215. Considering the proximity to London there are surprising amounts of pleasant countryside for you to enjoy upstream of Shepperton.

6 A Taster

The famous landmark of Windsor Castle above the Thames is the dramatic start of this section, and from Windsor to another royal town, Kingston, water abounds in all directions. On both sides you'll see gravel-extracted lagoons or the embanked reservoirs holding London's water supply, most bearing royal names.

Inevitably there has been much suburban growth this close to London and you'll come across lots of riverside dwellings, many peeping through the foliage of weeping willows. However, from your initial route through Windsor Castle's Home Park to as far as Shepperton, you'll still find open meadows to complement the built up areas.

From Windsor you reach Datchet, where in the 1830s an old bridge, long since gone, was rebuilt by Berkshire and Buckinghamshire since their county boundaries ran through the centre of the span. Perversely, Berkshire rebuilt their half in iron whilst Buckinghamshire used wood!

Runnymede, of such historic importance, follows before you come to Staines which, until man-made structures were built to impede the river's flow, was the upper limit of the Thames' tidal reach. Staines is ancient but very urban today. Passing the most impressive river loop along the whole Thames at Penton Hook your journey soon takes you onto Shepperton where an alternative route along the north bank is provided for the times when the ferry to take you across the river to Weybridge is not operating.

After a few kilometres the splendours of Hampton Court are reached. Pause before you get to the Palace to look at the bridge which appears to be old and constructed of brick and stone. This was however designed by Sir Edwin Lutyens and built in 1933 of camouflaged concrete. It's just a short distance from Hampton Court Park to Teddington Lock, beyond which the Thames is now tidal, and then you are into London.

Maps

Landranger maps	175	Reading and Windsor
	176	West London
Explorer maps	160	Windsor, Weybridge and Bracknell
	161	London South

Transport Information

Rail Services: National Rail **T**: 08457 484950 or www.nationalrail.co.uk
or www.railtrack.co.uk

Bus Services: National Public Transport Information Service
T: 0870 608 2608 or www.pti.org.uk

Taxi Services

Place	Name	Telephone numbers
Windsor	Five Star Car Hire	01753 859555
	Silverline of Windsor	01753 880765
	Windsor Radio Cars	01753 677677
Egham	Egham Taxis	01784 433933
	A Line Taxis	01784 430609
	Arrow Cars	01784 436533
	Gemini Cars	01784 471111
Chertsey	Abbey Cars	01932 568055
Weybridge	AGM Cars	01932 858585
	Eden Cars	01932 830830
	222 Yellow Cars	01932 841222
Walton on Thames	Walton Station Taxis	01932 221484
	Swan Cars	01932 230830

Toilets at Locks

Bell Weir Lock, Egham

Shepperton Lock

Molesey Lock

Police

Berkshire   **T**: 01865 846000

Surrey   **T**: 01483 571212

6   A Taster

Hospitals

Slough	Wexham Park Hospital, Wexham Street, Slough **T:** 01753 633000
Chertsey	St Peter's Hospital, Guildford Road, Chertsey **T:** 01932 872000
Kingston	Kingston Hospital, Galsworthy Road, Kingston **T:** 020 8546 7711

Tourist Information Centres

All provide an accommodation booking service

Place	Address/Opening Hours
Windsor	24 High Street, Windsor SL4 1LH **T:** 01753 743900 (general information) **T:** 01753 743907 (accommodation enquiries) **F:** 01753 743904 **E:** windsor.tic@rbwm.gov.uk www.windsor.gov.uk **Opening hours:** Summer (Apr-Sep): Mon-Sun 10:00-17:00 Winter (Oct-Mar): Mon-Sun 10:00-16:00
Kingston	Market House, Market Place, Kingston KT1 1JS **T:** 020 8547 5592 **F:** 020 8547 5594 **Opening hours:** All year: Mon-Sat 10:00-17:00
Richmond	Old Town Hall, Whittaker Avenue, Richmond TW9 1TP **T:** 020 8940 9125 (general information) **T:** 020 8940 0057 (accommodation enquiries) **F:** 020 8940 6899 **E:** information.services@richmond.gov.uk www.roomcheck.co.uk/rl (accommodation) **Opening hours:** Summer (May-Sep): Mon-Sun 10:00-17:00, Sun 10:30-13:30 Winter (Oct-Apr): Mon-Sat 10:00-17:00

The following towns on the path also have a wide range of services and accommodation:

Datchet, Staines, Walton-on-Thames, Kingston and Teddington.

For details contact the Tourist Information Centres.

EGHAM

TO0171   on path

Egham 1.2km (0.7miles)

Town with full range of services

Egham has a wide range of accommodation; details can be obtained from Windsor Tourist Information Centre. However, the accommodation provider below particularly welcomes Thames Path walkers

Runnymede Hotel & Spa

Mr Andrew Duggan
Windsor Road, EGHAM, TW20 0AG
T: 01784 436171 F: 01784 436340
E: info@runnymedehotel.com
www.runnymedehotel.com
130 £136.00 37 £136.00 2 £136.00 11 £68.00 ♀♂ ♿ V 🚭 ⊡ 🔝
Mastercard, Visa, Delta, American Express, Diners ★★★★ ⛰ ETC Silver Award. Various promotional tariffs available, please ask.

SHEPPERTON

TO0867   on path

Shepperton

Town with full range of services

Shepperton has a wide range of accommodation; details can be obtained from the Kingston Tourist Information Centre. However, the accommodation provider below particularly welcomes Thames Path walkers

Splash Cottage

Mr Malcolm Shaw
91 Watersplash Road, SHEPPERTON, TW17 0EE
T: 01932 229987 M: 07751 041055
F: 01932 229987 E: info@lazy-river.co.uk
www.lazy-river.co.uk
2 £45.00 1 £45.00 (£30.00)
♀♂(min age 9) V 🏔 🚭 ◆◆◆
⛰ Price includes continental breakfast; add £5/person for English breakfast

American Bar Association's
Magna Carta Memorial,
Runnymede

Hampton Court Palace

Section 7

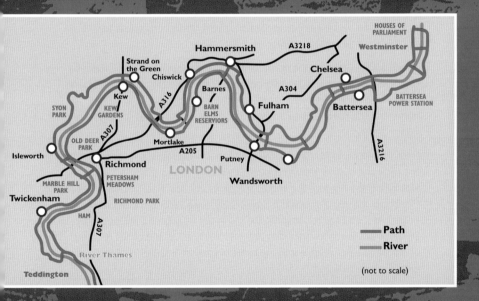

LONDON: Teddington to Westminster

You can choose to walk on either the south (32 km/20 miles) or north (34 km/21 miles) bank of the river as you head into the heart of London on this section. You'll find surprising amounts of greenery at the start, some impressive historic houses on both banks and old village settlements now absorbed by the city.

7 A Taster

Whether you walk on the south or north bank, or cross from one side to the other where bridges allow, there's a tremendous amount to see between Teddington and Westminster.

The first few kilometres of this section are remarkably rural as you pass through Ham Lands, Petersham Meadows, Richmond's Old Deer Park and Kew Gardens on the south, and through Marble Hill Park and Syon Park on the north. Best views of the looping river can be seen from Richmond Hill and you'll be in good company if you make the detour since many famous poets, writers and artists have been inspired from this spot for centuries.

Strand on the Green on the north bank is a miraculously preserved riverside community with picturesque fishermen's cottages and elegant period houses overlooking the river. Other old settlements like Richmond, Kew, Barnes, Hammersmith, Fulham and Putney still also manage to retain some flavour of village atmosphere.

From Chiswick and Mortlake to Westminster, the river is wholly urban in character but trees and bushes grow at the water's edge creating almost a linear park. Mortlake is the finish of the annual spring Varsity Boat Race between Oxford and Cambridge Universities which has been held since 1845 and starts downstream at Putney. At Barn Elms waterworks, the reservoirs have been transformed by the Wildfowl and Wetlands Trust into natural looking lakes and ponds to attract a range of birds and other wildlife into the heart of London. In 2002 a bittern, a rare bird indeed, chose to visit.

Elegant and expensive Chelsea on the north bank has been home for many famous literary and artistic people. Standing in Chelsea you'll look across the river to Battersea, your view dominated by the 1936 power station, now just an empty shell. Battersea used to be known for its asparagus beds, but most people now associate it with its dogs' home.

Your finish to this section could hardly be more impressive since you either stop outside or look across to the Houses of Parliament in Westminster, the seat of government.

Maps

Landranger maps	176	West London
Explorer maps	161	London South

Transport Information

Rail Services:	National Rail **T**: 08457 484950 or www.nationalrail.co.uk or www.railtrack.co.uk
Public Transport in London:	London Travel Information **T**: 020 7222 1234 or www.londontransport.co.uk
Boat Trips in London:	London Tourist Board's River Trips Line **T**: 0839 123 432

Police

Surrey	**T**: 01483 571212
Greater London	**T**: 020 7230 1212

Hospitals

Isleworth	West Middlesex University Hospital, Twickenham Road, Isleworth **T**: 020 8560 2121
Hammersmith	Charing Cross Hospital, Fulham Palace Road, Hammersmith, London W6 **T**: 020 8846 1234
Kensington	Chelsea & Westminster Hospital, 369 Fulham Road, Kensington London SW10 **T**: 020 8746 8000

Richmond

Tourist Information Centres

All provide an accommodation booking service.

Place	Address/Opening Hours
Richmond	Old Town Hall, Whittaker Avenue, Richmond TW9 1TP **T**: 020 8940 9125 (general information) **T**: 020 8940 0057 (accommodation enquiries) **F**: 020 8940 6899 **E**: information.services@richmond.gov.uk www.roomcheck.co.uk/rl **Opening hours**: Summer: (May-Sep) Mon-Sun 10:00-17:00, Sun 10:30-13:30 Winter: (Oct-Apr) Mon-Sun 10:00-17:00
Britain Visitor Centre	1 Lower Regent Street, London SW1 4XT (personal callers only) **Opening hours**: All year: Mon 9:30-18:30, Tue-Fri 9:00-18:30, Sat-Sun 10:00-17:00 (Sat 10:00-17:00 Summer)
London Tourist Board	Victoria Station (personal callers only) **E**: enquiries@londontouristboard.co.uk www.londontouristboard.co.uk **Opening hours**: From 8:00 daily

Other tourist information centres, for personal callers only, are located at:

Liverpool Street TIC, Liverpool Street Travel Information Centre, Paddington Travel Information Centre, Victoria TIC, Waterloo International TIC, Heathrow Airport TIC, Heathrow Visitor Centre.

LONDON

Hampstead Heath Youth Hostel

The Manager
4 Wellgarth Road, Golders Green,
LONDON, NW11 7HR
T: 0208 4589054 **F:** 0208 2090546
E: hampstead@yha.org.uk
www.yha.org.uk
⛄⛄ 🚭 🅷 Dormitories: £20.40/adult,
£18/child, breakfast included

Earl's Court Youth Hostel

The Manager
38 Bolton Gardens, LONDON, SW5 0AQ
T: 0207 3737083 **F:** 0207 8352034
E: earlscourt@yha.org.uk
www.yha.org.uk
⛄⛄ 🚭 🅷 Dormitories: £19/adult,
£16.75/child, no breakfast

Oxford Street Youth Hostel

The Manager
14 Noel Street, LONDON, W1V 3PD
T: 0207 7341618 **F:** 0207 7341657
E: oxfordst@yha.org.uk
www.yha.org.uk
⛄⛄ 🚭 🅷 Dormitories: £22/adult,
£17.75/child, no breakfast

Holland House Youth Hostel

The Manager
Holland Walk, Kensington, LONDON, W8 7QU
T: 0207 9370748 **F:** 0207 3760667
E: hollandhouse@yha.org.uk
www.yha.org.uk
⛄⛄ 🚭 🅷 Dormitories: £21/adult,
£18.75/child, breakfast included

Houses of Parliament

Albert Bridge, Chelsea

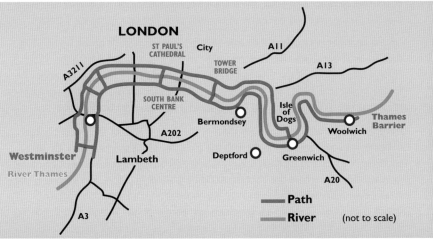

Section 8

THAMES PATH

LONDON: Westminster to Thames Barrier

This last section is relatively short, 19 km (12 miles) if you keep to the north bank or 18 km (11 miles) if you walk on the south side. Short it may be, but it's packed with the fascinating history of London. The Thames Path keeps next to the river wherever possible, but beyond Tower Bridge the banks used to be crammed solid with wharves and warehouses so that in places the Path currently has to detour away from the river.

So much to see and to explore in such a short distance! Too much, too, to give you anything here but a flavour of the London you'll be walking through. But, of course, there are numerous guide books about London for you to choose from and you can visit the London Tourist Board website at www.londontown.com

Your route from Westminster to the fabulous Tower Bridge on the north bank of the Thames is rich in the history of England's capital city. You'll pass, amongst other places, Whitehall, Cleopatra's Needle, the Inns of Court, the square mile of the City of London, St Paul's Cathedral, the Monument, London Bridge, several historic ships moored on the river and the Tower of London; all in just 4km (just over 2 miles).

On the opposite bank, along the same section, your route starts at the London Eye, then takes in the almost French atmosphere of the promenade beneath the National Theatre, great views of the City and St Paul's across the river, the massive brick former power station at Bankside, now the Tate Modern art gallery, Shakespeare's reconstructed Globe Theatre and Francis Drake's schooner the Golden Hind.

From Tower Bridge to the finish (or start) of the Thames Path at the Thames Barrier in Woolwich you'll be walking through the old heart of the working river. On the south bank you'll also pass Greenwich, where east and west meet either side of the meridian line and where the Millennium Dome is sited. In places the riverside is still crowded with decaying piers, wharves, warehouses and other paraphernalia of shipping, and there are still a few lighters and barges on the Thames. But the docks, mostly built in the 19th century to cope with the huge amount of ships unloading and loading their cargoes, are now redundant. Since the 1980s much of this landscape has been transformed by development, but there are still hidden corners for you to find and where you can try to imagine what it was like when London was the busiest port in the world.

Maps

Landranger maps	176	West London
	177	East London
Explorer maps	173	London North
	162	Greenwich and Gravesend

Transport Information

Rail Services	National Rail **T**: 08457 484950 or www.nationalrail.co.uk or www.railtrack.co.ukk
Public Transport in London	London Travel Information **T**: 020 7222 1234 or www.londontransport.co.uk
Boat Trips in London	London Tourist Board's River Trips **T**: 0839 123 432

Police

Greater London	**T**: 020 7230 1212

Hospitals

Vauxhall	St Thomas's Hospital, Lambeth Palace Road, Vauxhall, London SE1 **T**: 020 7928 9292
The City	Guy's Hospital, St Thomas Street, Strand, London SE1 **T**: 020 7955 5000
Dartford	Darenth Valley Hospital, Darenth Wood Road, Dartford **T**: 01322 428100

Tourist Information Centres

All provide an accommodation booking service except those marked ★

Place	Address/Opening Hours
Britain Visitor Centre	1 Lower Regent Street, London SW1 4XT (personal callers only) **Opening hours**: All year: Mon 9:30-18:30, Tue-Fri 9:30-18:30, Sat-Sun 10:00-16:00 (Sat 10:00-17:00 Summer)
London Tourist Board	Victoria Station (personal callers only) **E**: enquiries@londontouristboard.co.uk www.londontouristboard.co.uk **Opening hours**: From 8:00 daily

City of London Information Centre	St Paul's Churchyard, London EC4M 8BX **T**: 020 7332 1456 **F**: 020 7332 1457 **Opening hours**: Summer (Apr 1-Sep 30): daily 9:30-17:00 Winter (Oct 1-Mar 31): Mon-Fri 9:30-17:00; Sat 9.30-12.30
Southwark	London Bridge, 6 Tooley Street, London SE1 2SE **T**: 020 7403 8299 **F**: 020 7357 6321 **Opening hours**: Summer: Mon-Sat 10:00-18:00, Sun 10:30-17:30 Winter: Mon-Sat 10:00-16:00, Sun 11:00-16:00
Greenwich	Pepys House, 2 Cutty Sark Gardens, Greenwich, London SE10 9LW **T**: 0870 6082000 **F**: 020 8853 4607 **E**: tic@greenwhich.gov.uk **Opening hours**: Daily 10:00-17:00
Lewisham	Ground Floor, Lewisham Library 199/201 Lewisham High Street, London SE13 6LG **T**: 020 8297 8317 **T**: 020 8297 9421 **Opening hours**: All year: Mon 10:00-17:00, Tues-Fri 9:00-17:00

er tourist information centres, for personal callers only, are located at:

rpool Street TIC, Liverpool Street Travel Information Centre, Paddington Travel Information tre, Victoria TIC, Waterloo International TIC, Heathrow Airport TIC, Heathrow Visitor Centre.

 City of London Youth Hostel

The Manager
36 Carter Lane, LONDON, EC4V 5AB
T: 0207 2364965 **F:** 0207 2367681
E: city@yha.org.uk
www.yha.org.uk
☗ ⊘ ☖ Dormitories: £24/adult,
£20/child, breakfast included

 St Pancras International Youth Hostel

The Manager
Euston Road, LONDON, N1
T: 0207 3889998 **F:** 0207 3886766
E: stpancras@yha.org.uk
www.yha.org.uk
☗ ⊘ ☖ Dormitories: £24/adult,
£20/child, breakfast included

Rotherhithe Youth Hostel

The Manager
Salter Road, LONDON, SE16 1PP
T: 0207 2322114 **F:** 0207 2372919
E: rotherhithe@yha.org.uk
www.yha.org.uk
☗ ⊘ ☖ Dormitories: £24/adult,
£20/child, breakfast included

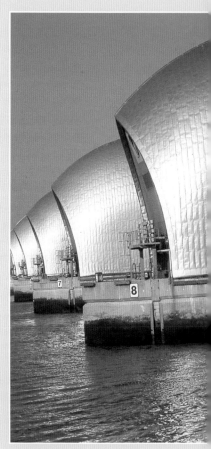

The Thames Barrier

Index of Places

Distances between places along the Thames Path in kilometres

The chart below shows distances (in kilometres) between places from the source of the River Thames to Teddington. Distances in London have not been included since walkers can choose to walk on either bank of the Thames and these distances vary.

From \ To	Source	Cricklade	Lechlade	Newbridge	Oxford	Abingdon	Wallingford	Goring	Reading	Henley	Marlow	Maidenhead	Windsor	Shepperton
Cricklade	19.7													
Lechlade	37.0	17.3												
Newbridge	63.1	43.4	26.1											
Oxford	85.6	65.9	48.6	21.2										
Abingdon	101.4	81.7	64.4	37.0	14.5									
Wallingford	123.3	103.6	86.3	58.9	36.4	20.6								
Goring	134.4	114.7	97.4	70.0	47.5	31.7	11.1							
Reading	151.5	131.8	114.5	87.1	64.6	48.8	28.2	16.5						
Henley	166.5	146.8	129.5	102.1	79.6	63.8	43.2	31.5	14.4					
Marlow	180.1	160.4	143.1	115.7	93.2	77.4	56.8	45.1	28.0	13.0				
Maidenhead	192.5	172.8	155.5	128.1	105.6	89.8	69.2	57.5	40.4	25.4	11.8			
Windsor	203.1	183.4	166.1	138.7	116.2	100.4	79.8	68.1	51.0	36.0	22.4	10.0		
Shepperton	225.2	205.5	188.2	160.8	138.2	122.5	101.9	90.2	73.1	58.1	44.5	32.1	21.5	
Teddington	242.9	223.2	205.9	178.5	156.0	140.2	119.6	107.9	90.8	75.8	62.2	49.8	39.2	17.1